Go Independent

The essential guide to becoming an
independent consultant and maximising your
relationship with your client

How to turn £16k into £400k!

Nigel James Hunt

Go Independent

A catalogue record for this book is available from the
British Library.

ISBN 978-0-9928469-0-9

Published by Smallholding Publications
For more copies of this book, please email:
nigel@crestwayconsultants.co.uk

Designed and Set by Smallholding Publications
Printed in Great Britain.
Cover designed by Early Bird Graphics

Acknowledgment/Dedication

I would like to dedicate this book to my wife for all the encouragement she has given to me during the completion of this book and thank all those that been involved in its publication.

Contents

Preface

I will share with you how to turn £16k into £400k from your assignments. That's right! You too can turn your independent consultancy or interim management business into a successful business model. I will share with you how to do this over the course of this book.

However, let's get one thing straight from the start. This is not a get rich quick scheme. You can and will reap high rewards for your work, but it is a given that you will already be experienced in your particular field of interest. This book won't teach you how, for example, to be a management consultant, programme/project manager or business transformation/change management expert, but it will show you, from my experience, how to conduct yourself as an independent consultant and business owner in your dealings with your clients and how to achieve the optimum return from your assignments.

If you want to achieve glowing testimonials for your work, winning repeat business, always be on the top of agencies and head hunters hit lists and be seen by your peers as an expert in your field, this book will help you along the way.

The way you present yourself and work with your clients is very important. We have all heard how it takes just a few seconds for someone to judge you when you meet them for the first time. In this time, the other person will form a lasting opinion of you so you will want this opinion to be managed, in other words the opinion you want this person to have.

I can hear you are thinking, 'manage someone's opinion! How do I do that'?

Be prepared beforehand.

That's right; preparation is the key to any first impression. Firstly, make sure you have done your research and have a clear idea before you meet anyone, who they are, what their background is and if possible how they behave. Based on this research you can tailor your approach to them and be someone with whom they feel comfortable. Having said that, never under any circumstances be unprofessional or act in a way that would compromise your principles.

Again, this book will help you present yourself to potential clients in the best way possible to secure the assignment or contract that you are bidding to win.

Along the way, I will also provide you with some personal anecdotes; useful links to articles, books and websites that will help you achieve your personal and business goals, so look out for these.

I will also show you how I use social media and other such websites to generate business leads and interest in my work.

So let's get started.

Introduction:

My name is Nigel Hunt, and I have been an independent consultant for over 15 years practicing in the field of business process improvement and change management, as either programme/project manager or management consultant, specialising in the field of working capital finance, the supply chain and general finance accounting. I have over 25 years of experience in the commercial finance, credit risk and receivables arena at senior management level with a number of blue-chip organisations having a global coverage.

I have completed over 20 key project management assignments in my time as an independent consultant which has benefited my clients to achieve hundreds of millions of pounds of savings to their profit and loss accounts and tens of millions of pounds of capital savings through process improvements, system implementations and change management activity.

Although I had a very good career as an employee of some large well known and respected corporations, all of which I thoroughly enjoyed and gained valuable experience , I can truly say I've never been happier than the day I set up my own business and started taking control of my own destiny. Many assignments and clients on from my first start in 1997, I have built up a vast knowledge of subject matter and have established myself as an expert in my field by keeping close to my principles of the utmost professionalism and integrity and by listening to my clients' issues and demands.

What I will share with you in this book is how not only to conduct yourself as an independent consultant or interim manager but also how to turn you assignments into lucrative periods of work. The subtitle of this book, 'How to turn £16k into £400k,' is a real example from my own experiences of working with client's over the years, and how you can extend your period of an assignment in order to reap the rewards on offer, but by doing so with integrity and professionalism and still offering your client's value for money.

Over the next chapters we will explore all aspects of how to run a successful independent consulting/interim management business including:

- Winning the initial client/assignment
- The negotiation tactics I use to get what I want
- Recognising other opportunities within a current assignment
- Re-setting client expectations
- Extending your current assignment
- How to conduct yourself
- Be seen as an expert.

Plus many more tips and advice on developing your business to achieve a high earning status.

For example, a senior management or even board level permanent role in a medium or a large corporation might net you between £70k and £150k per annum as a base salary. Well, as an independent consultant or interim manager I have consistently been at the upper end of this scale and much more, and I will share with you over the course of this book how you can also achieve these rewards.

What I have written in this book has worked for me. I see the contents of this book as my guiding principles, the way I have conducted myself in business over my career and by following these principles, the response from clients and peers has been extremely positive, and I have never had any difficulty in obtaining glowing testimonials and recommendations for my work.

Now I would like to share with you my guiding principles to enable you also to achieve your potential and increase your earning potential.

Section 1

My story

My story:

So, how did I get into independent consultancy in the first place?

Like a lot of people, my first foray into independent or interim working was after I was made redundant from my employer. I had already had a good early career in commercial credit and risk management working my way up through the ranks to become a European Credit Manager with a global distribution company. This was a role that I revelled in as it satisfied my preferences for strategic thinking, process improvement and change management. Also, like a lot of people being made redundant, I did not have a nice big pay-off so the need to step straight back into work was imperative.

During my initial search activity for a new role in credit management, I received a call from an ex-colleague who had moved to a competitor some months prior to the business going under and ceasing to trade. Having worked previously together to build up a first class credit and risk management team changing the attitudes of the business to embrace our philosophy of giving good credit not bad credit had helped the business grow to be one of the leaders in our industry. They recognised that my immediate availability was a significant asset and one that they wanted to secure. As a result, this call leads to a meeting over lunch and my first independent role.

This was a very exciting time for me, to be working for myself under your own terms of reference (albeit negotiated with the client) and principles made much more sense to me and sat much more comfortable with the way I wanted to work, *more recognised professional than a mere employee.*

So in 1997 I set up a limited company and started trading as an independent consultant. I had always worked and thought a bit differently to your normal company employee, I suppose I was passed down my Great Grandfather and Grandfather's entrepreneurial spirit and drive to be true to myself.

My Great Grandfather set up a market garden business between the first and second world wars and with his four sons was very successful owning three nurseries and landscape gardening business. On his retirement, he decided to emigrate to Australia and three of his sons went with him to replicate the business over there. The fourth son, my Grandfather, decided to stay in the UK and take his chances on his own. So he set up his own landscape gardening business and started trading sometime during the 1950's, and ending up having a star studded client list in and around the London area and building garden exhibits at the Chelsea flower show for some of the great gardeners of the day.

Unfortunately for me he died when I was young, and I didn't really get to know him that well. What I do remember though was a quiet, shy man with a great work ethic and highly professional in whatever he did. I was also often told, when I ask about him in later years, that he kept his own council and never talked about his clients other than professionally and about the job at hand. He was also a true gentleman and took particular pride in his personal presentation and work, something that I took to being the only way to operate in business as well as life in general.

So, what of the other sons that left for Australia? Well, they were also very successful landscape gardeners, the eldest sons only recently died, aged 98 and 99 years. It would seem that they had a good life in Australia!

So back to my embryonic business venture and how I developed my consulting practice and won more clients by following my guiding principles.

As I sat down with my ex-colleague at lunch in a local restaurant it dawned on me there and then that this was the time to make sure, I negotiated hard and got what I wanted out of the discussions. Although the business was not won at this stage it was the client who had contacted me, and that gave me the stronger negotiating position at the outset, although they may not have seen it this way!

Once we had got through the small talk and caught up with each other's lives (both of which are very important tools as you will learn later on in this book) we started the negotiations.

Although I was new to running my own business and selling my products and services my long standing commercial business experience meant I was already well aware of some of the basic negotiation techniques such as:

- Listen
- Let them make the first offer
- Use the flinch
- Aim high
- Defend your price
- Persistence
- Be prepared to walk away.

The above list is not meant to be an exhaustive list of negotiation techniques, but a list of those techniques that I already had experience of in my previous business dealings and those that I used to effect in my first few client negotiations. Later on in the book under the negotiations section I will deal with these in more detailed.

So using these negotiation techniques I agreed with the client the terms of reference for the assignment, the initial timeframe the assignment would last and the fees and charges that I would charge for my services. I'll list these again because although they seem simply they are important and we will come back to these later in the book:

- Terms of reference
- Assignment timeframe
- Fees and charges

So having agreed the terms of reference it was time for my first day on assignment.

First day:

On my first day of the assignment and my first day as an independent consultant, I realised that this was where I belonged and made my mind up there and then to make my new found career work. Cut loose from company politics and the sometimes straight jacket of being an employee, I set about the task at hand with great vigour and was determined to deliver high quality work and professionalism in all my dealings with the client's staff, company employees and its customers.

I acted with great care and diligence when it came to my interaction with the company's directors, employees and customers. I was aware that although I felt I knew how to act in my new capacity, others were not so sure how to, thinking I was just another temporary employee from an employment agency. This first assignment was to prove ground-breaking for me as it put into practice my long held beliefs about the impressions you give others and how this paves the way to a successful career and how not being seen to be an employee of a company by both the senior management and staff elevates you to new heights of professionalism and status. As long as you follow some basic rules, that is. So I will be coming back to this in the guidelines later on in the book.

One book that I've found is an excellent read and suggest that you get a copy of is, 'The Concise 48 Laws of Power', by Robert Greene and Joost Elffers. This book has some key tips on how your presentation to others has a lasting impact and how you use this can be very powerful indeed.

So back to the assignment!

This first assignment lasted for four months and resulted in the terms of reference being successfully delivered on time and within budget. The client was very satisfied with my work, and I would pick up a recommendation, as a result.

I was off to a good start and on my way to being a successful independent consultant.

Many more assignments followed:

Following the success of my first foray into being an independent consultant, I was buoyed up with confidence and ready for the next challenge. However, then it dawned on me. Where was the next client going to come from and how was I going to secure them?

I'd made the first and classic mistake any budding business makes. I'd concentrated so hard on making my client happy and doing an excellent job for them that I'd forgotten to keep up regular networking of my contacts and key employment agencies.

This was the first and only time I'd make this mistake. I cannot emphasise enough the importance of building, developing and regularly contacting your network is in building up and winning business. I now use several different ways to develop my network, and I will share these with you later on in the book.

What I will say now on the subject of networking is, it isn't easy, or at least I didn't find it easy. It is something I had to learn and my initial forays into group face-to-face networking where to say the least scary! Although I am now well practiced at networking I still find it a chore but I have long since realised that the chore is worth doing and doing regularly as a lot of business comes from networking.

Over the course of a year, I probably spent as much time networking as I do on client assignments. This, as well as being recommended for doing excellent work has meant that I have had relatively little downtime during my 15 plus years as an independent consultant.

I've mentioned downtime above, and this is always a big concern for any would-be independent who wants to break free of the corporate treadmill.

However, don't let this stop you realising your goal of becoming your own boss. If after doing your networking you are still struggling to find the next assignment then use this time to your advantage by:

- Keeping up to speed with the latest innovations in your particular field and industry
- Promise yourself to learn something new everyday
- Do your own research, either surfing the internet or reading books and other related material
- Expand your knowledge into other areas of interest to make yourself more sellable to clients
- Always be on the lookout to expand your network in the most unlikely of ways and places
- Participate in or instigate online discussions that are specific to your specialisation or interest, such as on LinkedIn, Twitter or create your own blog.

During a couple of months of downtime I had recently, more by design than anything else, I researched into a couple of other ventures, notably, buying and selling on eBay, and writing eBooks on various subject matter that hold a particular interest for me.

While doing this research, I made an effort to attend a number of seminars where I met some great people, and so tapped into a whole new network of individuals and organisations that will benefit my core consulting business, and just possibly send my business into some interesting and different directions.

As I mentioned earlier, you should never stop networking. Your network just like computer software needs constant updating and refreshing to get the best out it. While some of your core network may never change, there will be those individuals and organisations that drop out or become tired. Your network is a very organic entity and needs careful management.

So having got up to speed with my networking responsibilities, I was able to win a number of further client assignments with some notable names in the top FTSE500 businesses of the time.

I am not going to list the names of these organisations due to one of my professional principles of client confidentiality, even if I have not signed a confidentiality agreement with them.

However, I will list the industry and nature of the work as a point of reference to add value to the later chapters in this book:

- Credit reference industry, interim management
- Financial services, interim management

- Food retail, process improvement consultancy & project management
- Information technology manufacturing, process improvement consultancy & project management
- Information technology distribution, interim management
- Consumer electronics retail, project management
- Telecommunications, process improvement consultancy
- Service industry, project management
- Online betting and gaming, programme/project management
- General manufacturing, strategic/process improvement consultancy & programme/project management

As you can see from the above list of industries I have performed both interim management roles and acted as a consultant or project/programme manager. Over the time of being in business, I have tended towards replacing interim management roles with specific consultancy assignments or project management roles related to best practice process improvement. This is a personal choice and one where I feel I can offer the best value for money to my clients based on my experience and knowledge.

Over the course of my assignments, I have built up my knowledge and experience to a degree that my last two assignments have brought about the basis for this book.

A recent assignment won through the help of a head-hunter was a case in point.

I received a call from the head-hunter agent one afternoon giving me brief details of the role they had been asked to fulfil. The details where initially light in detail and as you will see later, it is very important to capture as much detail as possible upfront from an agent or client to make a judgment on the assignment, so as not to waste your time on a wild goose chase for an assignment that would not fit your profile or preferred way of working.

However, the initial details looked very promising, and I was interested. The next step was to arrange a meeting, through the agent, to meet with the board directors of the business in need of my services.

The meeting was set up, and a flight was booked to meet with the client. At the initial meeting, it was clear that the client had an open issue to resolve and although they had an initial view on how to tackle this, they were open to suggestions on changing some aspects of the approach required. They were looking to the expert (me) to review their approach and offer advice and guidance to put together the terms of reference. Following this first meeting, a subsequent telephone conference call was held to review and confirm the terms of reference for the assignment and discuss the fees and expenses that would apply to the initial timeframe.

I will refer to the negotiations in more detail in a later chapter, but I can say that my fees and expenses demands were accepted, and a change to the time and location details was agreed for both immediate and future changes to the assignment as necessary. All these negotiations where done with the utmost professionalism taking into account the clients current requirements.

Well, a month later I was flying out to the clients centre for operations to begin the project management assignment.

The initial timeframe for the assignment, laid down in the terms of reference, was for four months.

However, after several days in my role as project manager and while setting out the project timeline and deliverables, it was clear to me that four months was not realistic if the client wanted to achieve their goals. As a professional project manager, it was incumbent on me to point this out at the outset of the project and begin to change their expectations with a reasoned debate.

We will discuss later on in a later chapter that changing expectations are a vital tool to the independent consultant/interim manager.

As a result of my early intervention, it was agreed that the terms of reference would be altered. These altered terms would take into account the new information and the period of time the assignment would last, an increase from the initial 4 months to 12 months, in addition to this, extra resource would be given to the project in terms of project interim heads to support the new initiatives.

So we had not even completed the second week of the project, and we had changed the clients' initial expectations, extended the assignment and won added resource to the project to reach the deliverables set out in my project plan. Not bad!

Extending the assignment should always be your number two goal, after your number one goal which is to deliver results and value for money to your client. The two do go hand in hand.

Let's recap on the two top goals:

Number one goal = deliver results
Number two goal = extend the length of time of the assignment.
Delivering results is the life blood of the independent consultant or interim manager.

How many times have you been employed in a business or heard employees of a business complain that they cannot get things done because of entrenched positions (empire building) or attitudes (change unwelcome).

As an independent, you are above these internal company politics and entrenched attitudes, and seen by those who hired you as someone to break down barriers, and so are in a much better position to be able to deliver results. When I say, 'deliver results', I don't just mean the end game, but those little wins and results that push along your project agenda. These you should make sure that you shout from the rooftops, making sure that the widest audience possible and of course the CEO and CFO, your project sponsors, are made aware of how much you have achieved and how valuable your contribution is. I can guarantee they won't be getting these communications form anyone else in the business as regularly as you. So another valuable top tip is:

Top Tip:
Be seen to be delivering something at least every two weeks.

This could be as simple as a presentation on new business policy recommendations for example.
So now we had agreed on a new set of terms of engagement, the project was up and running at full steam. While I was reviewing the current process for one area of the business, I discovered that something was not right. I got this verified by one of my senior project group and we brought it to the

attention of the CFO. Again, I'm not going to give details of the nature of the issue due to client confidentiality but suffice it to say it had a major impact on the project deliverables and which resulted in the assignment being extended again this time from 12 months to 18 months.

Jumping forward to the close of this assignment, the adjusted deliverables were achieved and the project a complete success. The success of this project enabled the client to have confidence in the new processes and make significant savings on their bottom line profit and loss account and by significant I mean tens of millions of pounds.

So another top tip from my experience is:

Top Tip
Don't stick so close to the terms of reference that you miss out on other opportunities to make process improvements and change working practices.

And

Top Tip:
Always highlight process deficiencies as soon as you have verified them to the senior management of your client.

Another recent assignment won through the help of a longer established agency relationship is another example of taking a short term assignment and turning it into a long term project management role.

I'd recently moved house following a 2 month vacation, to rest after a particularly intense project management assignment, and still unpacking boxes my agent called with the news of a 4 week assignment overseas. The client wanted a review of key business processes to verify concerns identified by the current CFO.

This time the details of the assignment where very clear from the outset and it was clear that the client wanted the person to be based in one of its offices overseas and to do quite a lot of international travelling around its global network of offices.

However, although this role fitted my expertise to a tee and sounded very exciting, the timing and the extensive travelling did not fit my current circumstances. Our family had recently grown by one and with a 2 year old daughter and a 10 week old son my wife would not thank me being away from home for extended periods of time.
The decision was made there and then; I would turn down the opportunity this time and have a look for something else with less travelling.

Thinking that was that I assumed the client would look elsewhere. Well, a couple of days later, I received a further call from my agent to say that the client was still very keen to meet me, and they would be prepared to at least discuss the travelling requirement. With the agreement of my wife, the date was set for the meeting.

The meeting day arrived, and I had a good discussion with the client and it was clear that my knowledge and experience were exactly what they wanted, but we still had the travelling situation and the based overseas scenario to work through and conclude.

My negotiating position was clear. I could and would not be based overseas, and I could not and would not agree to extensive travel away from home. So that was that. The meeting ended on good terms, and we both knew where each other stood. I once again thought that would be that!

Well to my surprise a few days later I received a call from my agent, and they wanted me to join them and they would agree to me working from home with only a couple of overseas trips of overnight stays.

Another one in the bag!

Later on in the book, I will give you more details of how this negotiation was achieved, and the assignment won.

So that brings us up to date and has given you a flavour of some of my experiences of being an independent consultant or interim manager.

I have to say that over the last fifteen or so years' business has been good. It would seem that whenever I worried about where the next assignment was coming from, my network would work its magic, and I would get a call from my agents or other contacts and another assignment would present itself and negotiations would begin to win the business.

Now that I have been successful, this success has enabled me to have more free time to develop other ventures and to spend more time with my family, who are very important to me. It has also enabled me to put a bit back into my profession, which in reality has been a recent phenomenon. When I was working back in the late 80's and early 90's there were very few independent consultants and interim managers from which to learn. Today we find ourselves with an ever growing band of professionals taking the step into independent working from all types of industries and backgrounds.

Someone the other day asked me why I thought this was and I answered with the following comments:

I thought professionals were becoming disillusioned with the corporate lifestyle and the benefits (or lack of) that it now offered its employees. They were consistently telling me that they were having to work longer hours for less money and that their benefits were being cut and re-shaped so as to be of negligible benefit when taking into account the increased tax burden now applied to them.

They also were particularly vocal about not being valued by their employer and having the feeling of being taken for granted and expected to work longer hours, in effect overtime, for no reward.

Gone are the days when if you worked for a large corporate employer in a management position you would receive excellent peaks, like cheap to run company cars, first and business class travel, luxury office accommodation including your own office and secretary.

Another big change in businesses today and over the last 10 years or so has been the drift towards off-shoring large areas of the back office functions into shared service centres. This once large local back office functions would have employed a lot of junior, middle and senior managerial positions which are simply no longer available locally.

So of course we cannot forget the march of technology and the ability to automate vast swaths of the business processes that were once manual or at best semi-automated.

So if you are one if these employees, disillusioned with your employer or have fallen foul of the off-shoring phenomena or automation and want to tap into the rewards of running your own business and being your own boss, then I hope through my experiences and knowledge of running my own independent consulting business, I will show you how to act and help you win more business. It's my way of giving something back to our growing number of professionals embarking on their journey as an independent consultant and business owner.

I wish you all the very best of luck with your venture. As I have proved if you have a go and put your all into making it work, success is within your grasp. I'd like to say 'guaranteed', but nothing in life is guaranteed!

Good luck.

Nigel Hunt

Section 2

How to win business

Introduction:

In this section of the book, we will be looking at winning business for your independent consultancy practice, and how this can be achieved via different routes to market and utilising sound marketing techniques that I have pick up along the way that has helped me gain some impressive results.

Finding and winning new business:

The ability to find and win new clients is an essential skill to learn for any independent consultant/interim manager. This new skill may come naturally to some and not to others but is something that will build with practice and experience over time.

Finding and winning new clients doesn't have to be a daunting process, and I have found that some simple rules can be applied to achieve real success in building your client list. Before I go into my simple methodology I will share with you the areas I concentrate on to find and win new clients:

- Agencies and headhunters
- Direct with client – cold calling
- Other consultancies and practices
- Networking groups
- Referrals

The very first step in winning any new client assignment or project is to get your foot in the door. There could be tens or hundreds of independents vying for the attention of the client, and at this stage the client will typically only connect with 3-5 independents from the overall group. You need to find your way into that smaller group that gets past this initial stage.

Purpose — the overall purpose of this initial stage is for the client to weed out the poor quality independents and narrow it down to a few people to look at further. For an independent, the purpose of this stage is simply to get noticed and appear to be a good fit for the clients business and issues.

How to win — to win this stage you need to do several things. First, put your best foot forward. Your resume needs to convey your skills and experience clearly and on as few pages as possible. Be as professional with your resume as your would be in front of the client. At any meeting make sure you are polite and show your best work. Second, you need to be personal. The best independents will only respond to job ads where they can offer a personal response that is tailored to the individual client. Form letters tend not to work well.

Finally, there's always the option of cheating! If you know someone in the organisation or have another connection to the client, use it. A good referral will let you pass right by this initial stage and onto the next one.

Agencies and head-hunters:

On becoming an independent consultant or interim manager running your own business, it is easy to dismiss the need for recruitment agencies and head-hunters as being useful only for employees. I have found that until your network has been fully set up and even then, agencies and head-hunters are an invaluable resource for finding new assignments. In fact, a number of agency contacts are in my extensive network and are excellent information resources. Of course, you will have to find the good ones.

Once you have found the good ones, and you may need to network with fellow independent consultants and interim managers to find out who they are, and those that specialise in interim assignments, in your chosen field of expertise, you will need to register with them and it is best to meet them so that they can fully assess your credentials and so market you to the full to any potential clients.

Once registered and you have met with the agent or head-hunter and to be seen as an expert i.e. the agency sees you as on the top of their list of specialists, you will need to establish a strong relationship with the agency and no-doubt have completed several contacts with them, so they gain confidence in you.

However, to be on top of the list it is not essential to have done work for a particular agency before, but you will need to show that you have completed several successful contracts and if these have been time extended, then that's all the better. There is nothing better than showing an agent or head-hunter that you are a profitable resource (interim) and therefore worth investing time and energy in marketing extensively to their client list.

Once established as one of the top consultants or interim managers on the agencies list you will be in prime position to receive first refusal on any new assignments that the agent receives. I have found myself, through hard work and networking, to be on the top of a number of agents and head-hunters lists and regularly receive calls with interesting opportunities, not all of which will be of interest to me.

However, your network kicks in when you can tell the agent of someone else that may be better suited or if you are already on an assignment, someone who is available. There is nothing better than being able to help out fellow independent consultants and interim managers that are in your network. You will then receive the same service in return.

Top tip:

One very important aspect of dealing with agents and head-hunters is to make sure that they are fully aware of your resume. Make sure that your resume is fully up to date and is focused on relevant information only (there is no need for padding, just pinpoint your key experience and skills) and markets you effectively. Don't think of your resume as a simple CV, it is your main marketing tool so spend time getting it right, and you will reap the rewards.

Top tip:

Another tip is to identify and comment on future plans (i.e. make sure they know if you have decided to move into another area of interest that may not be immediately evident from your past assignments) and communicate this to your agent or head-hunter so they can add this to their search criteria.

An example of this is when I won an assignment as a project manager in banking and treasury when a look at my past experience this would not be immediately evident to the agent.

One thing that I stand by in my experience as an independent businessman is that although niche can be good and reap high rewards you have to make sure you can adapt to client requirements. There's no point turning down assignment after assignment because you do not play in that particular field.

Learn to adapt.

For example let's take the singer, Madonna. A global superstar who has managed to stay at the top of her profession for more than 20 years because she recognizes different trends and musical tastes and then adapts her act and music to play in that new field. It may be very subtle, but it works and has kept her music current. This could also be said for any number of artists but the outcome is the same.

Therefore the message is:

Don't sit on your laurels, kept learning and adapting.

Winning the client:

In this section, we will be looking at the various methods I have used successfully to win new clients.

I have previously mentioned these methods earlier in this section but to remind ourselves here they are again:

- Agencies and head-hunters
- Direct with client – cold calling
- Other consultancies and practices
- Networking groups
- Referrals

We will first take a look at winning new clients through our dealings with agencies and head-hunters and then move through the other methods.

One thing to keep in mind is the section on 'Qualifying a Lead'; mentioned in the first example, as this will be a common theme for all the subsequent examples, so I have only mentioned it once.

So let's get started:

Agencies and head-hunters:

Here we will be looking at the main elements of winning the client utilizing your relationships with your agents or head-hunters to maximize your chances of a successful outcome for both parties.

Meeting the client and winning the contract:

- Qualifying the lead
- The interview
- Your experience
- Presentations
- Your approach

Qualifying the lead:

It is very important always to qualify the leads you receive from your agents and head-hunters (or any source for that matter). All too often you get a call from an agent to say that they have this wonderful role that you are perfect for and before you realise it, you can be wasting valuable time and resources updating your resume specifically to this role and meeting the agent only later to find out that the role is either not what you thought or is outside of your specific expertise or requirements, be it specialisation, fees or location.

Therefore, you must qualify the lead by asking lots of key questions from the outset to avoid wasting your valuable time and resources on what was a red herring!

So what questions do I ask agents (or anyone for that matter) to qualify leads? I will now share with you my list of questions that has served me well over the years:

Qualifying questions:

- Are they exclusive?
- Are they talking to the decision maker or human resources?
- What is there influence with the decision maker?
- Is the position or project signed off or approved?
- If it is not signed off when is this going to be likely?
- Who is sponsoring the project?
- Is there anyone else already on the project?
- Are you talking to any other independent consultants?
- How many CV's have gone into the client to date?
- What is the decision process?
- What is the feedback process?
- What are the decision makers' criteria?
- Do you have a details job or project specification?
- What is the job or project time line or length?
- What are the fees (i.e. day rate or fixed fee) being discussed by the decision maker?

- Where is the job or project base location?
- Is the client open to remote working?
- If the job or project is terminated what is the notice period?

The above list of qualifying questions is by no means exhaustive but gives you an idea of what is required to be asked if you want to qualify a lead to a satisfactory point that you can make a decision to either continue to pursue it or politely walk away.

Next we will look at the interview with the agent.

The interview:

The interview, or rather the client meeting (as I like to think of it) is obviously key. However, you need to do your research very carefully and thoroughly both from your discussions with the agent and your own research into the clients business and their strategy.

When discussing the role with the agent you need to get them to be open and upfront with you on what the client is looking for and to align your expertise accordingly.

However, make sure you don't just sit in your comfort zone, challenge yourself and go for assignments that push your own experience into areas that mean you are out of your comfort zone; after all, this is the only way to keep your skills and marketability high.

Also have the confidence to challenge the norm in terms of working location and time as the client may not have thought of the different options available, but rather looks at their interim requirement as every other permanent role they recruit.

A recent assignment I successfully pitched for and won originally wanted someone based in their London and Dublin offices but in detailed discussions it turned out that they were quite happy for the resource to be based anywhere. I delivered this assignment while working 80% from my home location. The old saying, 'if you don't ask you don't get', applied with this company.
So don't be afraid to ask the key questions that are important to you!

Your experience:

You need to take the time to review you previous work and extract examples that fit the client's requirements. Remember, you will need to showcase to the client that you have delivered successful projects on time and within costs.

I recommend that, on this point, you don't go into great detailed but give the headline points and don't over egg your achievements.

Delivery, as you will see later, is very important to your continued success as an independent consultant.

Something very close to my heart!

As a successful independent consultant, you will already possess confidence in your abilities, but remember your prospective clients' don't know you so impress them with professionalism, good attitude and hold your head up high.

You run your own business so meeting a CFO or CEO of the client organisation is your peer group, you are not subordinate. They are a client not an employer.

So don't forget this!

Your approach to interviews and presentations:

I'm not going to go into interview techniques as this will have been honed over a number of years and experience but all I will say on the matter is look and sound credible, use presentation material and technology if it helps but not as a gimmick. I've found that unless asked or you are pitching for a particularly complex piece of business it is not necessary for winning the contract.

If a client does request to see previous work make sure you de-select any company names and sensitive data from the presentations and summaries the project and deliverables as necessary. Even if you have not signed any confidentiality agreements with previous clients, it's just the right thing to do. It's your professionalism at work.

Always present in the PowerPoint medium.

So you've been successful and won the client over to the extent that they are very interested to get you on board to deliver the project. However, don't congratulate yourself just yet. Now there is the negotiation of terms to get through yet!

Direct with client – cold calling:

Winning business by directly engaging with a targeted client is possibly one of the most satisfying experiences in becoming an independent consultant. All the hard work in promoting your services and the effort to convince them that you are the right person to trust with their issues and money has paid off, wow!!

How do you feel?

Great!

So you should because you have now found the winning formula, and that is a priceless lesson to have learned and one you can now take forward and replicate over and over to win more and more business for yourself.

That's not to say that every time you replicate your success that you are going to win but at least you can trust in your formula and put it down to experience and try to win next time.

There are many great reasons for going direct and not using the services of a recruitment agent or head-hunter but the key ones are:

- Negotiate bigger fees without any cut taken by the agency

- You own the client and can foster the relationship and benefit from any future business need
- There are no time consuming agency interviews as it's just you and the client
- You are more in control of the outcome of the eventual work that you will be performing for your client rather than getting it third hand
- You are more likely to grow your business and be billing multiple clients than if you simply rely on agency arranged work.

We will explore the above in a moment, but I particularly wanted to first focus on the last item in the list above.

Growing your business:

I've picked this one out for some special attention because it is the one thing that will turn your one man independent consulting practice into a much larger practice. How large? Well, that all depends on your ambition because even the big practices all started as much smaller concerns. I think what I am trying to get across to you is that by taking a step and the effort to seek out direct client relationships, it will foster the thoughts and opportunities for further business in areas that you may not have thought you could ever tap into and win.

For example:

You may have won a piece of work to review a part of the businesses internal processes and during or following your completed report or presentation to the client it was felt that a new piece of hardware or software was required. The client will naturally ask you first if:

a) Can you provide this service? Or

b) Do you know of anyone else that could provide the service?

Rather than at this stage turn around and say that you have no experience in this area I would rather say a big YES to a) above!! Then worry about the HOW afterwards. After all this is how businesses grow from small acorns to big oaks. Anyway, more of this subject later.

This is when you can utilise your extensive network of contacts, and you probably already know someone in your network that could help you deliver this or know someone that knows someone.

Once again this provides a great example of why networking and keeping your network fresh (and in this example, technically fresh) is so important in building up your business.

Now we go back and look at the other points:

Negotiate bigger fees:

As we all know, the agents can take upwards of a 20% fee of the negotiated day rate or fixed fee agreement which by any token is a sizable proportion of profit that you are missing out on that could be retained within your business. The only way you are going to achieve a proportion of this is to go direct to clients to win business.
Just imagine what 20% of a fixed fee, of £25,000 looks like! That's an extra £5,000 pounds for your business. On an extended twelve month assignment with a day rate of £650, this could be as much as £30,000 over the lifetime of the assignment.

So you can see that having in your armoury the ability to go direct to clients to win business can give you some significant rewards.

You own the client relationship:

One of the big benefits of dealing directly with clients is that you own the client relationship and can foster further dialogue and win addition business without first referring back to the agent or stepping on their toes if you try to talk to the client first.

On several occasions where I have owned the client relationship by winning business directly, I have won significant repeat business from them because I was there on the ground, able to see opportunities as they arose and have no barriers to talk directly and openly to the client to try and turn these opportunities into further revenue earners.

In addition to this, you start to develop your own list of contacts that will come in very useful as you develop your business further.

No time consuming agency interviews:

If you cut out even one extra meeting in winning an assignment over time, this would represent a great time and cost saving to your business. So to cut out any agency meetings is one further big plus for dealing directly with the client.

In my early days when I only won business exclusively through agents and head-hunters I racked up thousands of pounds of expenses travelling to and from meetings that could have been directed at other marketing actively if dealing direct with clients.

You are more in control:

For me, one of the main advantages of dealing direct with clients is that you are dealing with the decision maker and you are having first hand discussions on what that client requires to make the assignment or project a success. You are there at the beginning of the discussions and can influence and share the thinking around the business case of the work to be carried out and therefore be more in control and benefit from the eventual outcome than you otherwise would.

It is also a great way to start to re-set the clients expectations before you even win the business that saves an awful lot of time rather than going through this process after you have started on the assignment or project.

Be in control and stay in control.

Other consultancy practices:

I have found it particularly useful during my career as an independent consultant to foster good relationships with other consultancy practices, not just as a tool to find additional clients and win work, but also a means to broaden your appeal, exchange knowledge and share experiences.

You will find that once you have developed your relationships with the other practices you will hear of opportunities to help them out as a member of their team.

That's right; their team!

Under these circumstances, you will be part of their team and marketed as such to their client and as such you will be charging the consultancy practice for your time and expenses as it is not your client.

Often these opportunities come about when a consultancy practice does not have a particular expertise, or that they have the expertise, but it is already booked out to another client, and they need to fill the gap. This of course can work in the opposite way if you have a client that requires some expertise that you are unable to fulfil, and you have to fill it by finding resource from another consulting practice.

So I have found that making contact, networking and forging good relationships with other consultancy practices (the completion in most cases) has provided many benefits and a number of fee earning opportunities that I otherwise would not have had.

In fact, I currently sit on the 'bench', as it is commonly called, of five consulting practices and have a number of consultants from other organisations who sit on my bench.

By operating in this way, I have expanded my available market space, and my services offering beyond my own expertise, which has over time, provided me with some very valuable fee paying work that I otherwise would have missed out on if I had not innovated in this way.

Top tip:

So my advice to you is to get out there and network with your peers and competitors to expand your client network and service offering which over time will elevate your own organisation as one that 'can do' rather than 'can't do!'

Networking groups:

We all know more than ever the value of networking as there appears to be more and more networking groups and opportunities out there and growing it seems on a daily basis.

However, I 'm not going to recommend which networking groups are best, or to tell you how to network effectively; for the purposes of this section, we are looking at the opportunities within your current established networking groups for winning new clients.

I have been using various networking groups for a number of years and have found that opportunities can come from the unlikeliest of places. So my first piece of advice to you is not to restrict yourself to the most likely of networking groups within your field of expertise.

As an example, I once received a lead from a networking group that I beyond to that was centred on executives enjoying motorcycling rather than business. We were on a particular outing to visit the newly expanded Triumph motorcycle factory, when on admiring their manufacturing facility; I got talking to a member of another group on the same visit who happened to be riding the same motorcycle as me. Well, after admiring our respective machines, we got around to talking about what we did, and it so happened he worked for an organisation that was looking to make some significant changes to their organisational structure that fitted my skill set and knowledge perfectly. Suffice it to say that about 3 months of work, and negotiations later, I won the contract to act as their senior consultant during the initial phase of the organisations structural change planning.

Top tip

Don't limit yourself to the obvious networking opportunities.

Obviously, the more quality networking you do, the more opportunities you will dig up, but there has to be an element of fun in business too so find groups that also interest you from an outside of work perspective if you can.

Referrals:

In this context, I talk about referrals as being from persons or clients with which you have previously worked.

From my perspective, there can be no greater acknowledgement of your hard work than to receive referrals from past colleagues or clients. It makes me glow with pride and makes all the hard work worthwhile.

Referrals for me are, in effect, the result of putting into practice all that I have expressed in this book, the culmination of hard work, professionalism and the delivering of results, i.e. getting the job done.

I have had a number of referrals in my time, but there is no better compliment as a professional to get one in acknowledgement of your hard work and significant contribution to the success of an organisation from a CEO of a global business.

Bring on those referrals!

Negotiating the contract terms:

Introduction:

This is now the fun bit! It may seem daunting at first but at least you have been selected by the potential client to start negotiating, so that means you are now in prime position to win the business. It's not time to get cold free now!

I do not profess to be an expert negotiator, and I am sure there are many great sales techniques and books about the art of negotiating but what I am sharing with you here is what has worked for me.

Firstly, let's list the main negotiating tools, we discussed earlier, that have worked so well for me over the years:

- Listen
- Let them make the first offer
- Use the flinch
- Aim high
- Defend your price
- Persistence
- Be prepared to walk away

Let me say now that this book is not meant to be an authority on how to negotiate with clients, but more what has worked for me over the years. Remember, you can learn all the skills you want but you still have to develop your own style which will be different for everyone. Remember, this is my style, or take on the subject that I am sharing with you here.

I've listed above a number of tools that I have used as my negotiating guidelines, and each of these has formed the basis of my trusted technique.

Listening to your client is a key skill. Listening is a skill that needs to be learned and advanced. It seems that this skill is so often overlook and thought of as something easy and basic and of course we all know how to do it, after all we are experts, right?

Well, no we're not as it happens. The best negotiators are those that listen and who let others have their say first, without interruption, before making their case. That helps set up one of negotiation's oldest rules:

Whoever mentions numbers first, loses.

While that's not always true, it's generally better to sit tight and let the other side go first. Even if they don't mention numbers, it gives you a chance to understand what they are thinking.

One excellent article I think explains this brilliantly is 'The forgotten art of listening' by Ed Brodow (website www.brodow.com).

So, I recommend that you go and read this article for some more insight on the way to listen and to use this skill, which we all have but don't use effectively, to win more negotiations and business.

The other key skill to successful negotiating is aim high!

You are the best in the business at what you do, and the client knows this from their interaction with you, hence the offer to join them for the project. They know that excellence costs good money so don't be shy to make your first pitch a high one. Of course you have to assess the clients appetite for this type of expenditure, there is no point asking for £1000 per day if the client expectation is £500 per day. However, there is no harm in pitching in at £750 and realising £600 - £650 per day.

Expenses:

Don't forget to add in **Expenses** to your negotiations. I have always managed to get the client to except full expenses as part of any package. The chief reason for this is that it's a future unknown expense so is not immediately visible. Remember though never to abuse the expense in such a way to contravene many of the client's principles.

However, this does not mean you cannot use first class rail or business class flights if the clients own employee rules dictate otherwise. Remember you are not an employee!
However, you also have to bear in mind that sometimes macro-economic conditions dictate that you may have to be more sensitive towards the subject of expenses and the client's policies and rules on travel, etc.as not to cause any offence.

For example: since the global banking crisis hit in 2008 most companies have revised their internal employee expenses policies and have, therefore, been much more aware of getting value for money form external resources such as ourselves and expenses are at the forefront of negotiations at the present time. I have had several occasions since the banking crisis where clients will only deal with negotiations on a fixed fee leaving expenses out of the negotiations altogether. It is then down to your own pricing policy to determine how you negotiate the fixed fee to cover some or all of your perceived expenses and therefore, determine if the contract/assignment is going to be profitable and worth winning.

Time:

The other main area for negotiation is **<u>Time</u>** in the client office versus the ability to work off-site (at a home location). For my last two major contracts as a consultant/programme manager, I've been able to negotiate working from home for the majority of time i.e. working in the office 2 days per week, in one and working from home 80% of the time in the other. So again don't be afraid to ask. Remembering again to assess the clients business and what they are asking you to do before negotiating in this point.

I've found that if you have a good home office set-up with high speed internet access and good computing you can do most things from a remote location. I have run a global process improvement implementation programme for a FTSE 500 company from a home location with only infrequent visits to HQ and other sites both in the UK and abroad.

You also must stick to your bottom price or fee. After pitching your initial fee and if this has been rejected I would refuse to go lower than my minimum fee (In my case, a set minimum daily rate).

Top tip:

Remember at all times to take into account the costs of running your business and the expense necessary to perform the contract or assignment in question. After all, you are in the business of making a profit and you must have a clear idea at all times of your profit margin.

Always be prepared to walk away from the assignment if the terms of reference cannot be agreed or if anything is not to your satisfaction. Obviously, only you will now what you will or won't except, but at all times do not jeopardise you professional principles and integrity.

Now that you have successfully negotiated a contract with the client, it's time to get started.

Keeping the client happy:

Keeping your client happy is your number one objective. However, this does not mean at all cost; i.e. do not jeopardize your professional integrity to keep a client happy.

It really should go without say but be professional and courteous to the client and everyone you meet during the period of your assignment. It may also be necessary to comply with some of the clients' health and safety requirements or particular policies and procedures while you are on site, so make sure you assess these before the assignment begins and if you have any objections make them know up front.

And of course the best way to keep a client happy is to:

Deliver on time within the terms of reference and on budget.

Along the way to delivering a successful assignment or project, there will be plenty of opportunities to show the client that you are managing the work effectively, efficiently and adding value.

The main way to do this is to deliver things regularly throughout the project period. You may say that the delivered element is all at the end, and that is the main goal.

However, in between then and now there will be opportunities to deliver small pieces of work, identifiable quick wins, additional process improvements presenting themselves, evidence of works done to date (i.e. project charters, issues logs, project status reports, project presentations on progress, etc.) and of course the regular project communications and workshops giving you plenty of media to show everyone that you are on top of the project and progress is being made.

Used effectively and regularly these should be enough to make any anxious CEO or CFO feel comfortable that you are in control.

At the end of the day, the last thing any CEO or CFO wants to hear is problems with an independent consultant or interim manager, after all you were brought in to help him or her improve a given situation and not be the subject of complaints or rumour.

Top tip:

Never let yourself be compromised in any way by giving others in the organisation the opportunity to muddy your name because mud sticks and you will be out on your ear before you can say 'independent consultant'.

Communication is the key:

Regular communication on the progress of the assignment or project and early communication on any issues is so important to build trust with your client and to make sure that any souring of the relationship is avoided.

You would be surprised at the amount of times I have seen a lack of communication and efficient escalation of issues has resulted in problems for other consultants and project managers in the past.

I'm not going to go into any detail here about how to communicate or what your communication's strategy should be but simply put it to you that regular, timely and effective communications with your client is so important that you should invest some time in researching this as a separate topic.

Make sure your client knows your terms and conditions:

This sounds obvious, but it is worth making sure that your client fully appreciates your terms and conditions for doing business both generally and for the assignment or project. This will mean that there are no surprises later on once you are working with the client that could derail your relationship.

There is nothing worse than a contractual dispute that pits you against the client as these kinds of disputes can get ugly and often the client's legal department gets involved. This is very much best avoided at all costs.

To avoid this scenario ever coming up make sure that everything is up front, clearly stated and understood from the outset. It is worth spending a bit more time at the start of the negotiations agreeing the business terms and conditions and the assignment or project brief to avoid any misunderstandings. You definitely want to avoid terms and conditions issues being raised halfway through your relationship.

Top tip:
Make sure your client knows your terms and conditions of business so that any conflicts are dealt with before the assignment starts. This will avert any disagreements later on.

At the end of the day keeping your client happy, will be as a result of all your efforts. Firstly, at the outset in the negotiations and signing of the contract, then as you work on the assignment or project through regular communications, delivery and by being seen as someone that the client can trust and wants to have as their confidant.

So to conclude:

- Be open in your negotiations and each party fully understands the terms and conditions of business and the terms of reference for the work
- Deliver on promises
- Communicate regularly
- Escalate issues effectively
- Win your client's trust.

You should then have a happy client!

Extending your initial contracted period:

One of your main objectives must be to extend your initial contracted period as this is the obvious why to increase your business and the one where you can influence the outcome from a position of authority.

Why?

- Reap higher rewards
- Build your credibility in the profession
- Build up strong business relationships with agents and head-hunters
- Add value for money to the client (this one sounds odd, but I will explain my thinking behind this).

Earlier in the book I made mention of an example where I had successfully secured a time extension to the original assignment terms of reference. I will now share this one and other assignments with you in more detail.

First, let's remind ourselves of the scenario:

After several days in my role as project manager and while setting out the project timeline and deliverables, it was clear to me that four months were not realistic if the client wanted to achieve its goals. As a professional project manager, it was incumbent on me to point this out at the outset of the project and begin to change their expectations with a reasoned debate.

As a result of my early intervention it was agreed that the terms of reference would be altered to take into account the new information and the period of time the assignment would last was increased from the initial 4 months to 12 months, in addition to this extra resource would be given to the project in terms of project interim heads to support the new initiatives.

This highlights the importance of having the ability to both recognise and change the clients' expectations about the tasks and time needed to complete the assignment or project.

Don't miss read this as an 'at any costs' requirement. If, in this assignment, I was genuinely able to complete the project within the 4 month time frame, then that's what I would have done. We're talking about recognising when the clients' expectations are clearly over optimistic and being able to articulate this to the client professionally, with the relevant facts and figures and sensitively. There is no point saying to your client that they've got it all wrong, and you need double the time to complete the tasks.

Remember the client isn't wrong, but rather they have not been made aware of all the facts and figures to have made their decisions and what you are providing to them are those additional facts and figures to enable them to reconsider their decisions and if necessary change the details of the terms of reference for the assignment.

That's why it is essential that as part of your assignment or project you are responsible for putting together and presenting a project plan to the client.

I have a basic but very effective methodology when beginning a new assignment or project and I will share this with you now:

My simple project (assignment) methodology:

- Project (assignment) charter
- Business case for the project (assignment)
- Project (assignment) plan (including resources)
- The issues log
- Issues and risks management
- Escalation management
- Data gathering
- Client interviews and documentation
  - As is process flow diagram and documents
  - To be process flow diagram and documents
  - SOP documents (standard operating procedures)
- Project documentation version control
- Regular presentations
- Regular communications

This methodology is one that has stood me in good stead for the last 15 years of assignment/project management. I have based my methodology on a number of different assignment and project scenarios over the years and found what ultimately works for me.

If you want to go into more detail about the world of project management, there are hundreds of books on the market about being a successful project manager and one that I particularly recommend is 'The project Manager', mastering the art of delivery, by Richard Newton, published by Prentice Hall Financial Times. Another useful book to read is 'The project management life cycle' by Jason Westland and published by Kogan Page.

Both these books deal with the project management profession but present it in very different ways, two good additions to your book shelves.

Anyway, back to the project plan:

Your first step towards extending the contract is, in fact, at the very beginning of the assignment when putting together the assignment or project plan. If the client's hands you are pre-worked project plan suggest that this is re-worked so that you can add your knowledge and experience into the plan (I've never found this to be a problem and only once did a client suggest I use their project plan, which, by the way, I politely refused).

If you are doing an interim management assignment which doesn't have a specific requirement for a project plan, then I suggest you put together a work plan with the client to establish the delivery (or targets) time frame in addition to the terms of reference.

By formulating your own project plan you will establish in detail the time frame and resources necessary to complete the project. I've found that with dedication and hard work this can be achieved within a 3 day window, so pretty quickly you will be able to present to your client the basis of the project deliverables and the need for any revisions to the original time expectations.

In terms of the project plan presentation, I will leave this up to you. However, I use either Microsoft Project Manager or Microsoft Excel depending on the size and complexity of the project.

By the way, I haven't forgotten about the other project methodology items on the list, and I will review all of these in a further chapter, in the book.

Another key step to extending your assignment with your client is to become 'temporarily indispensable'. Before I discuss this I want to share another recent assignment example with you:

Again let us remind ourselves of the scenario:

I'd recently moved house following a 2 month vacation, to rest after a particularly intense project management assignment and still unpacking boxes my agent called with the news of a 4 week assignment overseas. The client wanted a review of key business processes to verify concerns identified by the current CFO.

Now this assignment is an example of one that under the initial terms of reference was deliverable within the 4 week time frame. As agreed at the end of the 4 weeks, I delivered a presentation to the board on a full review of their end to end processes for a function of their business. This presentation was, as they say, in the trade, a quick and dirty review.

Having said that, it was still a thorough piece of work; taking into account interviews with senior employees, extensive data gathering and my own observations, and then formulating these into a 20 page PowerPoint presentation.

The trick here of course is all in the presentation and how you offer up the action items to flow from your recommendations, as the expert, and the alternative scenario for taking no action.

Now you need to put your sales hat on and deliver a persuasive argument to the client to take the recommended actions and present yourself as the ideal person to head up and lead the project henceforth. So that's how I completed my first 4 weeks assignment and ended up delivering the project at the end of week 70!

So in the two examples above we can see the different scenarios that resulted in extending the assignment:

1. **Changing the clients initial expectations**
2. **Follow on work through your recommended actions.**

I've found in my experience that quite often both scenarios will play a part in securing an extension to an assignment, particularly in the case of the first assignment example. Here, we not only changed the clients' initial expectations on the assignment time frame, but also identified other areas of concern and provided a persuasive argument backed up with facts and figures and real examples to the client that meant to take no action would not be very palatable. In this example, the argument to take positive action to change was accepted as a matter of urgency.

So now we come to the third key tool for extending the assignment.

- **Making yourself temporarily indispensable**

This of course is very much based on your ability to deliver the key stages (milestones) of the assignment on time and with the desired results but also to be seen to be delivering. We mentioned earlier in the book the need to keep the client updated with regular communications on your progress and other activities such as workshops and presentations.

During my time as an independent consultant I make sure I do the simple things very well, and then go that extra mile to make the client feel comfortable that all is well and they do not need to worry about the project as it is in very safe hands.

Let's face it CEO's and CFO's have many things to worry about, and if you as the independent consultant or interim manager (project manager) can manage the situation, so they do not have to worry about you and the project they will be very happy and more open to suggestions from you about the projects direction, resources required and see you as an expert in terms of the project deliverables and timetable.

At the end of the day, you must get into the Zone (as I call it) where they see you as a peer, an expert and a key confidant. That way they will feel comfortable and then happy to leave you alone to get on with the project. You will have been accepted as part of the 'Golden Circle', meaning those whom the decision makers can trust. Once you get yourself into this position, they will also be more interested in keeping you close by for as long as you can prove invaluable i.e. indispensable. Now, we all know that being indispensable is not an infinite situation, so ride the wave while you are in this position.
For an example:

During a project management assignment, I quickly recognized who I needed to impress at board level and by reaching beyond the original project terms of reference (as a side project), I uncovered some additional process weaknesses in the organisation and recommended the project terms of reference be extended to capture these. This was a surprise to the individual and eventually saved them multi-millions of pounds. This also elevated me to the 'Golden Circle' and I became indispensable for the period of the assignment. Bearing in mind that this assignment was extended from 4 months to 18 months representing a revenue increase of approximately £200,000 pounds!

Another example:

While I was working for a client as a project manager, I recognized that there were areas of the business that the current employees did not fully understand and appreciate the importance of key processes. I, therefore, made sure I became the expert and made myself temporarily indispensable.

Having made myself, temporarily indispensable the initial 6 month assignment was extended to 17 months representing a revenue increase of, again, approximately £200,000 pounds!

So you can see there are various ways to make yourself temporarily indispensable and once you've done that of course you are in a prime negotiating position to discuss assignment extensions and future project work.

Over the course of my experience, I have extended the initial assignment time frame in all but two cases, and both of these were down to personal choice to complete the terms of reference as agreed in the initial negotiations. Having calculated the extra revenue this has brought in over that time, let me tell you it is significant and therefore has been very much a key part of my ongoing business strategy. Not only is it a great way to generate additional revenue for you but it also gives you great credibility with agents and head-hunters as they can see the benefit in retaining you as their first point of call for any new assignments, and making sure they supply you with assignments that have the potential to be long term.

Remember, great business for you and great business for them.

Remember:

In the two examples above that I have shared with you the additional revenue to my business was approximately £400,000 pounds.

Top tip:

Make the agents want to do business with you, because you offer them the best profit solution.

Delivery and adding value:

I have already touched on delivery and adding value in the previous sections, but I want to make further comment on the importance of this in a separate section.

Delivery:

I mention earlier about the importance of regular communications to your audience on the projects progress, so let's remind ourselves what these were:

'small pieces of work, identifiable quick wins, additional process improvements presenting themselves, evidence of works done to date (i.e. project charters, issues logs, project status reports, project presentations on progress, and workshops) giving you plenty of media to show everyone that you are on top of the project and progress is being made'.

In other words, everything you do to progress the project or assignment can in some way or other, however small, be classed as '**delivery**'. It is up to you to make sure that your targeted audience is regularly updated on your progress i.e. he who shouts loudest!

Delivery is all in the mind...

What do I mean by this? Well, I mean that your client will have a view on what delivery means for the project or assignment and no-doubt this will be the delivery of the end game, the successful conclusion of the project 'deliverables' and 'Milestones' as agreed at the outset in the 'terms of reference' or for non-project based assignments the 'work plan'. However, as a project manager we're not going to leave the success of our project until the end game as this will leave us open to criticism from others, regarding perceived project progress and value for money type questions.

No, we are going to make sure that everything we achieve, be it big or small, ground breaking or mundane will be publicized as project progress or **'on-going delivery'**.

I am reminded of a recent project management assignment where I published, in addition to the normal weekly project update report, details of process improvement initiatives in the format of a 'white paper*' even if these would have been covered in the main project delivery mechanism.

This should not be taken as a rouse, but more a vehicle to make sure that your targeted audience can see the progress as it happens and get that comfort factor we spoke about earlier, happy in the knowledge that the project is safe in your hands.

(A white paper is an authoritative report or guide that helps solve a problem. White papers are used to educate readers and help people _make decisions,_ and are often requested and used in politics, policy, business, and technical fields. In commercial use, the term has also come to refer to documents used by businesses as a _marketing_ or _sales_ tool. Policy makers frequently request white papers from universities or academic personnel to inform policy developments with expert opinions or relevant research. A Wikipedia definition.

So to recap:

Delivery is anything you do on an assignment or project that you feel will elevate you and your expertise to show how indispensable you really are.

- Regular communication
- Regular and timely presentations
- Additional information formats such as white papers and articles for the clients' internal employee newsletter
- Reports
- Workshops
- Day to day wins, and issues that have been raised and resolved.

I have tried to make sure that I delivered a presentation at least once every two weeks on various subjects to keep my visibility high up on the list with the senior executive.

Adding value:

This is one of the main reasons why I became an independent consultant. The ability to add value to a client's business is so satisfying personally and so rewarding for your business.

While I am not saying that you cannot add value as an employee of a business, you are generally held back by either the businesses policies and procedures or your bosses, or both!

How often do your hear that someone's ideas have been thwarted by another department or the boss as taken the credit for adding value! Well, as an independent consultant you are at the forefront of the good idea, or the business changes and therefore you will be in a position to push through the good idea and you will get the credit for delivering the changes.

Now that's very satisfying.

So what do I mean by adding value?

Adding value by:

- Adding actual or achievement value
- Adding perceived value, being that safe pair of hands
- Bringing people and groups together
- Bringing your experience to the problem (being able to identify improvements where others cannot see the wood for the trees).

The above short list is only meant to be an example of what adding value means to you and your client. A definition of adding value could be as follows:

'Extra feature or features of an item of interest (product, service, person etc.) that go beyond the standard expectations and provide something more while adding little or nothing to its cost'. Wikipedia.

In our work, adding value is more than the end game or conclusion of the project deliverables. It is about the finer touches, the professionalism and the integrity that you bring to the assignment.

Taking the above list that I suggested, the actual or achieved value is going to be all the things that can be measured e.g. a process change, whereas the perceived value is going to be the intangible items as mentioned above, your professional attitude and experience, your integrity and ability to see things others cannot and your impartiality. Don't underestimate these as items as added value, they will be the ones that get your assignment extended, getting recommendations and keep you winning further assignments.

The other two suggested items, bringing people and groups together and bringing your experience to the problem (being able to identify improvements where others cannot see the wood for the trees); I am reminded of a great passage in a book I recommend that you add to your library. The book is 'My years with General Motors' by Alfred P. Sloan JR.

There is a passage in the book that for me perfectly illustrates where your professionalism, integrity and experience in bringing people together and seeing problems that others do not can add significant value to your client's organization. It may be seen as intangible, but it is a very important skill that you should have in your armory and for me is more a greater skill than the job of getting the assignment done, after all this is your bread and butter skill.

So to recap:

The intangible values are:

- Professionalism
- Experience
- Integrity
- Ability to see things others cannot
- Impartiality
- Bringing people and groups together.

Delivery of results is obviously the key to a successful assignment or project, but by making sure you add value as an independent consultant is what marks you out as someone who will get noticed, and will enable you to win repeat business with your client and receive recommendations to others for future work.

So let's go and Add some Value!

Re-setting client expectations:

The first thing to get to grips with once working with your client is to tackle the tricky subject of re-setting your clients expectations. Now this is not to say that in every case, you will have to go through this exercise but I have found this situation occurring in most assignments or projects I have worked with over the years.

Obviously, whether you come up against this situation will depend largely on what type of work you are doing for your client, but rest assured in my experience the expectations of most clients, if there is a lack of a detailed project mandate and/or business case in place from the beginning of your association, is largely underestimated in terms of the time it will take, the resources required and the costs involved in a project or assignment of works.

To recap the common underestimations are:

- Time it will take to deliver the benefits
- Resource required to commit to a project
- Costs involved completing the project within the desired time and with the set deliverables to reap the stated benefits.

To show you this in a little more detail I will share with you an example of an assignment I was involved with where all three of the above underestimations where evident and so required me to quickly re-set the clients expectations before the project could get started on any meaningful footing:

Example:

With this particular client, there was no initial proposal process as they had come across my details via a recommendation. Normally a client would expect to follow a more formal proposal process setting out the particulars of the assignment or project in detail before awarding the contract. However, in this case, following an initial chat about their business and the issues they had it was agreed by both parties they could work together, and the start date was penciled in the diary.
This particular client suggested during our initial chat that the issues at hand, while irritating and needing to be fixed, were not business critical.

On arriving at the client site and initiating several high level discussions with the senior management, it was clear to me that the issues effecting the client's business while irritating had, in fact, already become business critical and the whole emphasis and direction of the project needed to be changed and enhanced to the reflect this change in status.

It was now down to me to convey this in no uncertain terms to my client and begin the process of re-setting their expectations on a big scale in all of the points made above.

How to go about re-setting expectations?

In this example and with identifying the business critical nature of the issues I decided to convey my concerns to the senior management which had brought me in, this more a matter of courtesy than anything else, to present my concerns and offer them some key facts from my analysis. At this session I also said to them that it would be best practice in this case to brief the senior executive at the businesses Head Quarters, to give them the benefit of studying my findings and to have the opportunity to agree any changes to the project brief (given how light it currently was).

Using my powers of persuasion and charm (after all they had brought me in as an expert and person who would fix their issues!) I gained unanimous agreement to publish my finding to the board of directors. Due to the business critical nature of the issues it was decided to aim for a specially convened board meeting to be set up in two days-time. This gave me just enough time to refine my presentation of the facts, and to hammer home the message. And the message let's not forget, was not that the issues where business critical (although they were) but the need for a

Re-setting of expectations!

Key lessons:

Although you have been brought in as an expert to help fix the issues never forget that you are also running your own consulting business, and it is important to make sure you can run on your agenda as much as possible. It is also important not to miss out on any extended or future business opportunities that may present themselves however small. At this stage I wanted to clarify what I mean by *'let's not forget, was not that the issues where business critical (although they were) but the need for a Re-setting of expectations!'*. I mean that, for this meeting, it was not really about the actual business issues under discussion but the outcome of the meeting that was important. Remember that you have a peer group now at senior executive level and as an independent consultant you need to do more than just deliver the work; you need to be seen as a key influencer of the outcome. This is how you will earn the big money.

At the board meeting, I presented my findings and after some tough questioning from the assembled audience it was agreed that the initial time, resources and costs where underestimated and needed to be brought up to date in light of the new information and enhanced business criticality of the issues.

So I was asked by the board if I would undertake the production of a comprehensive project mandate and business case documentation for the enhanced project to cover all the new information and present these back to the board, which had now appointed a steering committee, to review and agree to the new project direction.

As you can imagine this was quite a coup for me and was an endorsement of my decision to escalate the issue to the senior management and to the executive management rather than just accept the project or assignment at face value and start work on what the client thought, they wanted.

The result of this work on re-setting the clients expectations was to extend the initial project/assignment from 3 to 18 months (time), increase the project head-count in line with the new emphasis on the criticality of the issues (resources) and agree to a new enhanced budget to pay for the project (costs).

The conclusion of this example:

So you can see that you could just accept the clients view of the world and in this example work on the assignment or project for 3 months without being able to influence or fix the issues at hand, and to miss the business criticality of them, or now be project managing, with the full backing of the board, an 18 month project that would deliver real value to the client by fixing the business critical issues and solving their issues. This is when as an independent consultant you really start to earn your spurs!

The example given in this case also re-emphasizes what I said in an earlier chapter on 'Extending your initial contracted period' and another example of how you can turn an initial small fee paying client into a much larger one and thereby continue to build your reputation as an independent consultant that delivers results.

Don't just do what is expected, go the extra mile and deliver real value to your client.

Section 3

How to conduct yourself on assignment

Introduction:

Your conduct as an independent consultant or interim manager is absolutely fundamental in your ability to influence key decision makers and gather glowing testimonials and recommendations. As I have mentioned earlier in the book, being a successful independent consultant or interim manager is so different from being an employee of a business. You are not bogged down with the daily politics a senior position brings, and you are not subordinate to anyone, not even the CEO.

That's right! It may come as a surprise to some, but you are a peer of the senior executive management of your client and don't you forget it. This is one of the lessons that are sometimes harder than others to comprehend and master, but master it, you must, to earn the big rewards on offer in independent consultancy or interim management. I have consistently earned high rewards during my time as an independent consultant and a lot of this has been on a par or above that of the senior executive management.

You've won the assignment because the client can see you are an expert in your field, and you have already impressed them during meetings and conference calls, with or without a presentation.

However, the greater task at hand is when you start the assignment, and then you will need to impress all over again, but this time on a different level.

What do I mean by this?

Well, the impression you gave them at the 'winning the assignment' stage will be different on the actual assignment. During the initial business discussions on your suitability to win the assignment you were no doubt being judged against others; now you are the chosen one you will be being judged on your conduct, your communication skills and interaction with the senior executive and employees and of course results.

Under this spotlight, you must demonstrate the utmost poise and integrity and your demeanor most show one of total confidence in your expert status: Anything less and you will find it difficult to demand the respect of your new peer group.

Later on in this section I will talk about 'playing the king' which is so important. You must show that you can work within the senior executive sphere, not in an arrogant way but with calm professionalism and respect for your peers.

Top tip:

There is no place in the independent consultants' armory for being arrogant, cocky or outspoken in an overly negative way.

Play the king (look, talk and act the part):

Introduction

There are two states of mind that are essential for being a successful independent consultant. These are:

- Confidence is everything.

- You have to believe in yourself.

The above two phrases typify what a good independent consultant should believe and maintain in their minds. It is this that will get you through the difficult days and build your business success.

Being an expert and being comfortable with this in yourself is one thing, but being able to demonstrate this, strut your stuff so to speak, is something quite different, and some of you may need to work on this. It is so important to be comfortable acting like your peers and in our new independent status that means like CFO's and CEO's. I like to think of it as 'Being the king!' and I'll come onto this a little be later.

I've found that a particular way of dealing with this has worked for me, and although, over the years, I've polished up my act, in truth I was always of this mindset from an early age.

My mother likes to recount the story of the day when she picked me up from school, but was directed to collect me from the Headmistresses office. Upon collection, my mother was told that, *'now we have established who is boss'* I could be on my way.

So you see, from an early age I have had a healthy questioning of authority, and this has never left me. In my mind, I don't believe that anyone is better than me; we are all free spirits, and there are no boundaries to our possibilities. We all can be anything we want to be if only we can get rid of the constraints that this modern world wants to try and place on us.

What I am not saying is having no respect for authority or dignity towards others. What I am saying is that I have a healthy questioning of authority, and just because someone is in authority this does not automatically make them a better or more knowledgeable person than me.

With this in-built character trait from any early age I have always been comfortable dealing with senior people or authoritative figures; with the feeling of not being inadequate in any way.

During my earlier career I was only twenty when I took up my first managerial role and on my career journey was quickly promoted in various organisations until I reached a mid-senior executive level. During this time, I always felt very comfortable being around and dealing with the senior management.

One of my favourite tricks was to look closely at what the senior executives in the business where wearing, the shoes, shirts and suits and make sure that I too looked the part, even if it meant I had to spend £600 on a suit or £80 on shoes (prices back in the 1980's), which on my salary was no mean feat but I saw it as an investment in my future. I felt that it was essential not only for me to feel comfortable in their presence, but they would be comfortable in mine and treat me as one of them. Acting and looking the same sure seem to work for me!

However, if you are not as lucky as me then you will need to learn how to develop this skill to be more successful.

This brings me nicely back to a book I recommended earlier, **'The Concise 48 Laws of Power'** by Robert Greene and Joost Elffers and published by Profile Books Ltd.

The section: Law 34; 'be royal in your own fashion: Act like a king to be treated like one';

This section of their book demonstrates this philosophy perfectly and I recommend you get yourself a copy.

I hope this recommended section gives you a sense of what I mean and how important it is to give off a confident persona.

So, go 'Play the King', and fill your full potential.

Don't get involved in office politics:

If there is one piece of advice I will give you, it is this: never get involved in the office politics or out-of-office social scene. That's actually two pieces of advice!

One of your key drivers to have made you set out on your own and divorce yourself from the corporate rat-race was no-doubt distaste for the office politics, so don't indulge yourself now you are free from it. It may be tempting to get 'stuck in' to the office gossip and bemoaning of this and that, but remember, you are now above all that and must at all costs resist getting involved. You must maintain your integrity and pose.

I've seen a number of independent consultants, unable to resist the lure of a good gossip, come unstuck and leave profitable assignments early simply because they could not keep their own council. This is not only damaging to their pockets, but more importantly also their reputations.

Top tip:
As an independent consultant or interim manager, reputation is everything.

If you read any articles about how to deal with office politics, you will no-doubt be told not to keep your head down and in fact face it head on, get involved and win over or round the individual which has the power! While this may be good advice for those employees of organisations, I would avoid this tactic as an independent consultant.

Simply, you don't have to get down to this level. Remember, you have set out or help to set out the terms of reference for your assignment and have engaged with the senior executive of the organization, which see you has an expert, to advise and guide them to the deliverables. You, therefore, have a clear and specific mandate to act under and deliver, they are not looking for an employee relationship; they are (and you are) treating this as a business-to-business relationship so there is no need and no time to get involved in office politics.

I mentioned earlier that I have seen a number of independent consultants fall on their sword due to a lack of experience and because they couldn't resist getting involved. It reminds me of one such incident which I want to share with you:

While working on one particular difficult and intense assignment, where I was projected managing a piece of work, I had a number of independent consultants under my direction. One particular consultant was relatively new to this profession and our way of working and couldn't quite get to grips with dealing with the client on a business-to-business basis, having previously been employed in a corporate organization for a number of years, and due to this lack of experience got involved in a 'clique' which was seen by a senior executive as being particularly disruptive to a number of ongoing initiatives. I have to say at this point that the individual in question had no idea of this 'cliques' reputation but by association was earmarked as a co-conspirator. I'm reminded at this point of the old adage, 'be careful who your friends are'.

Anyway, back to the story:

Having been associated with a disruptive element in the business meant that this individual lost all credibility with the senior executive and the project team and had to fall on their sword.

Now, this was a shame because the individual in questions was excellent technically, but their mistake was that they thought there was no difference between acting like an employee and an independent consultant.

Rule: avoid the office social scene:

The other area to avoid at all costs is the office social scene. I've seen may a consultant get into a messy situation as a result of not following this rule. I'm not saying that you cannot be friendly and make friends with those in your clients' organisation but do it with care. I am also not saying that you should turn down every invitation you get from your client to dinners and events, but do choose which ones to attend and when attending never slip from your place of dignity and integrity. This doesn't mean be boring, but it does mean be extra thoughtful how you act and how you interact with those around you.

Some basic rules that I have applied to myself in these situations:

- Never get drunk, or drink too much
- Never be inappropriate with either language or action so as to cause offence
- Avoid uncouth jokes and anecdotes unless your audience is such that they would appreciate the humor
- Never put yourself in a compromising position
- Don't get into any arguments
- Never discuss politics or religion
- Don't be part of the late into night/early morning party crowd. Know when to leave.

Over the course of my career as an independent consultant I have been asked to a lot of office dinners, parties and events and by applying the above basic rules I have never had a problem. However, I do not accept every invitation, and I base each decision on its individual merits and the occasion itself.

For example, if the senior executive wants to invite me out to dinner to discuss the project performance and have a wind down and get to know you session, I would accept but be very candid about what I tell them, remember to keep your own council at all times!

Never get into a stand-off with a client over an issue or point of view:

Remember the classic sales phase 'the customer is always right'!

We all know that this is not always literally the case but in terms of your dealings with your clients it must be kept in mind when dealing with difficult and complex issue that divide opinion on the way forward for the project and or a set of outcomes.

There is nothing to say that you cannot have a difference of opinion with your client, but it is the way you handle it that will make all the difference, not necessarily to the outcome, but certainly in the way they view you and your professionalism.

Top tip:
You must separate your personal views from those of the clients' business requirements, its culture and vision they have for the business moving forward.

Sometimes the cultural restraints of a business or its long term vision statement may clash with your view of best practice and what has worked for you in the past but you must not let this cloud your judgment and make an issue of it and therefore get into a standoff with your client. A good independent consultant will view this as an opportunity to influence the situation towards their point of view rather than digging in their heels and sticking to their guns. You must learn to blend ideas and views into a workable and acceptable compromise for all parties.

I have always seen my role as an independent consultant to be both a subject matter expert and also an ambassador for balance and order. You probably thinking what is he going on about! Well, over the next few paragraphs I will endeavour to explain.

I like to call it my 'holistic' approach to work.

Holistic (adj) meaning (Holism. n) from The Collins English Dictionary:
'1. The idea that the whole is greater than the sum of the parts, that a system may have properties over and above those of its parts and their organization. 2. The treatment of any subject as a whole integrated system.

For me, this holistic approach means that I take a strategic view of the clients business and of the project I am working on and work with the client to implement the best solution in terms of best practice for procedures and controls within the vision and strategic direction of the clients business.

There would no point in coming and trying to take a business in a direction that it would resist going just because your ideas and system worked for a previous client. There is no way that I try to brow beat a client into taking my way is best at all cost style of approach. I feel more in control and feel that I can add more value when I am offering best practice that is aligned to the clients' strategic vision.

When I was a senior operational manager in a business some fifteen years ago, I would always seek to clarify what it was that the business .i.e. the board, were trying to achieve – their strategic vision – so that my department was step up, and its goals aligned to this vision. I found that it was the path that gave me most satisfaction and success when dealing with colleagues and the senior executive.

I would effectively take the corporate strategic vision and overlay best practice and controls to achieve the right blend and give me that holistic approach I am talking about here.

Alternatively, tread carefully, be professional and add value by coming up with a solution or solutions that suit both you and the client for the benefit of the assignment or project.

Keep a professional distance:

It is so important for an independent consultant to keep a professional distant from their clients.

I've touched on it before in this book, but I cannot overemphasize this point enough. Everything about being an independent business and its' whole point of being is to be professional, and have the highest level of integrity. This is the way I have set myself up to operate, and it is really what this book is all about.
So keeping your distance from the client is another way to achieve this.

Now, while we want to keep our distance we don't want this misinterpreted as being overly aloof and uncommunicative as this would be counterproductive.

However, what we do mean is that while being an excellent communicator and interacting with our clients in a positive, helpful and relaxed manner, this should be of a very high professional standard with the utmost integrity at all times.

There is no place for complacency. This will lose you clients and your reputation will be damaged.
So aspire to the highest level of professional conduct.

Section 4

The practical stuff

Introduction:

In this section, we will be looking at some practical things that any independent consultant is going to need to know and have in their personal tool kit for success.

These items discussed here have been used by me during my assignments to great effect and have formed some of the key foundations on which I work with clients and associates.

The items we will be looking at in this section are as follows:

- Social media and how this impacts us and how we use it to our advantage
- Presentations – advice on how to construct and deliver excellent presentations to clients
- Organisations to belong to and how these can benefit your business
- Project management methodologies – the simply one that has worked for me
- IR35 – a brief look at the implications and where to seek advice
- Take detailed notes when gathering information and data – why this is so important to focus on and get right.

So here we go:

Social media:

I have to admit that the whole social media thing took me a little while to grasp the purpose and importance of to business and the networking potential that it provides.

My wife is a big advocate of social media, but it took her a while to convince me of its worth. I now realize, and I would recommend that you have an account on LinkedIn, Facebook and Twitter, if you have not already done so. If you don't currently have an account set-up with these sites then I recommend you stop now and do it straight away.

Since I set up my accounts (a while ago now) I have seen the vast potential of networking and keeping in contact with business acquaintances and abreast of events that social media can bring. I'm not carried away with it you understand, but it is now a part of my business strategy.

While I was talking to a business friend of mine we discussed the importance of the social media medium and I remembered I'd seen this article:

Did you know that Sainsbury's, 'M&S', Dell and the BBC are getting real results from social media?

Do you think you might be missing out, or that social media is a waste of time?

Think again. Social media strategies are now a key part of unlocking success for any business – whatever its size. Social media can help you find new customers, keep old ones and network without leaving the office, plus much, much more! (Email article from chase chamber of commerce Feb.2011).

By social media, I mean Facebook, Twitter and LinkedIn to name the three main ones in popular use at the moment.

I have a business page on Facebook linked to my business website and utilize LinkedIn as my main online networking tool.

By having a business page on Facebook linked to my company website gives me a presence on the number one social network medium and, therefore, will capture any searches made.

With LinkedIn, I have found over the last year or so that it has enabled me to schedule in networking very easily as part of my daily administration routine and once set up is very easy to maintain and communicate with your network and groups.

The trick with these social media sites is to at least have a presence and over time work with them to build up more exposure and usability.

Over time, these networks will build up into an associate and client list with which to market your services.

At one time, I had over 50 groups that I was networked into on LinkedIn and while you can opt out of receiving updates to posts and news items I always felt it rather defeated the objective to opt out.

The key with the groups is to assess which ones are working for you and which ones aren't. Once you have established this you can deselect those ones not working for you and reduce the amount of unnecessary traffic through your email inbox.

Once you have a core list of network groups you can use these to comment on posts, post articles yourself or link presentations and video to promote your business and skill set (or as I like to call it, your brand).

I have found that LinkedIn is by far my most successful social media tool, but I would certainly not discount the others. I have recently realized that Facebook is becoming more important and for some people is replacing text messaging and becoming a sort of same time messaging tool.

Now, I am not in any way an expert on social media, so anything here is just my thoughts and experiences of using the main sites mentioned and how they have benefited me in my networking tasks, goals and administration.

If the reader would like to know more on this subject then there are plenty of books and articles dedicated to this subject.

If you look on Amazon.com, you will soon see a large number of titles from which to choose.

For those of us that are not social media savvy my advice is just to have a go and see where it takes you but always remembering that it is not the be all and end all in terms of marketing and networking.

It is a tool that compliments the normal and traditional marketing techniques, like sales literature and telesales.

Presentations:

Presentations are a necessary part of any independent consultants' armory. They are an extension to our sales and marketing strategies that can be and quite often are your best way of establishing your status as an expert in a particular field.

The presentations that you will deliver over time will showcase your work, ideas and strategies to the client and if done well will stand you apart from the crowd in what is a very competitive market place.

During my time as an independent consultant I have delivered hundreds of presentations but don't think you cannot reuse them to form your own suite of standard format presentations. Indeed I have about 5 standard formats that I have developed over time and reuse all the time.

Having your own suite of pre-formatted presentation material can save you a lot of time when taking on a new assignment and can give you that speed of response that a new client will be impressed by and quickly elevate you to the golden circle and temporary indispensability.

Top Tip:

Have a least two pre-prepared presentations formats ready when starting a new assignment.

My presentations:

All my presentations are in PowerPoint format and are either constructed with my own branded master file or with the particular clients branding depending on what the client wants.

I have never had an issue with either style unless the presentation is generic information then I make sure that it is branded with my company details and copyright. This is important as you may want to use these presentations later on in your own marketing material, as white papers or as free downloads from your website. Over time, you will build up a nice archive of material that you can draw down on and use when on assignments or when dealing with the press as expert articles or other marketing activity.

As I mentioned earlier, I have approximately five different standard presentation formats that I can use again and again and these fall into the following criteria:

- Base review presentation
- Project status (update)
- Project summary
- Road map
- Process documentation

These standard formats will enable you to deliver quickly, information to your client, and form part of your deliverables, as mentioned earlier, not just the end game deliverables, but every bit of information you produce that stakes your claim as an expert.

Below I have given you an example of a standard base presentation format so you can see what it looks like and how you might want to structure your own standards presentation formats.

Example of a standard 'Base review presentation':

- Agenda
- Scope of review
- Where is your organisation (or process) today
- How we did it (the review)

- Subject matter (or process) summary
- Data analytics & KPI measures
- What we found
- Suggestions for improvement
- Reporting recommendations
- How and when
- Road map (diagram)
- As is process maps
- Q & A (questions & answers).

As I mentioned above, this is my own standard format which I have found works very well but you may have a different idea on what works with your clients, but I hope you find this example useful.

The other standard format presentations in my list above follow a similar if cut down version of the above one tailored to suit the requirements of the assignment and client that you are working on/with.

Presentation delivery:

None of us like sitting through a dry presentation with a dry presenter flicking through a set of sixty overly wordy slides and simply repeating verbatim what is being shown to the audience.

However, the type of presentations you will be delivering as part of your assignment will have to be detailed and probably be of some length. So how do you get away from the scenario mention above?

If you must read verbatim off the slide deck then my recommendation is to format the presentation with animation. If you do this at least you can hold the audience's attention on the individually presented item. However, I would also recommend that you talk around each item or point as it is made as it is very important to interact with your audience as you do so.

I have found that a combination of tactics works very well when delivery lengthy and detailed presentations. These tactics have been tried and tested with my clients, and I will share these with you now.

Presentation tactics:

- Make sure your presentation is visually appealing (there's nothing worse than looking at a wordy black and white slide).
- Utilise animation but keep it simple (no need for flashy lights and spinning and swirls. Simple appearing is enough).

- Highlight the subject of what is to be discussed and then talk about the detail from the hip.
- Include lots of visual diagrams that explain what you are delivering.
- Offer the audience a chance to ask questions throughout the presentation, not just at the end.
- If it is a long presentation (over an hour), then have a break out session for refreshments.
- Use a prop if possible, like a pointing stick or laser light and a remote slide changer, so that you can move about easily while delivering your presentation.
- When speaking be heard and project your voice clearly (if in a large room or conference hall then you may need a microphone so make sure you find out in advance if one is available).

I am sure that you can think of a few more that you might add to the above list that work for you but this is my simply tactics that have successfully gotten me through some pretty heavy presentations with positive feedback from the audience and client. This, after all, is the objective!

Top tip:

Remember at all times when delivering a presentation to speak clearly, be heard and offer the facts in a visually appealing why while at all times engaging with your audience so that you don't lose them to boredom.

Organisations to belong to:

As an independent business, you will want to look at belonging to some organisations that will compliment yours and help you build your network and also show-case your work as an expert in your chosen field.
Of course any organisation you belong to must be ethical and be beyond reproach as you don't want to align yourself with any unprofessional or corrupt organisations.

Fortunately, most professional organisations you will no-doubt come across in your chosen profession should meet the above criteria but you will want to research each one to make sure it fits with your business and personal philosophy.

I particularly like the ones where you can get yourself on a panel of experts at a conference and immediately be seen by the audience as the go to person. The other good place to be is as a committee member of an organisation that can influence the particular industry or profession that you are in and have frequent exposure to the press, be it in trade journals or national press. If you can elevate yourself to the vice chair or preferably the chair then you are seen as a person who represents the organisation and therefore the authority on the area of or subject matter that the committee represents.

I have had many offers to join committees as both a member and as chair, but I have not always taken these up due to not having the available time. While it is very worthwhile taking up these offers you also have to balance your other commitments, be it business, other committees or family.

As a passed committee member and chair of one particular organisation, I found it particularly worthwhile from a personal fulfilment perspective and professionally. During my time as the chairman I was able to contribute to and front several professional contributions to trade and national press and attended many conferences in my capacity as chairman enabling me to meet lots of key figures in my profession and industry that certainly aided my networking and list of contacts. Several of these meetings and contacts ultimately turned into business opportunities and even long lasting friendships.

Top tip:

Don't underestimate the power of belonging to organisations and putting yourself forward to sit on the committee. It can really elevate your standing in your profession and industry.

There are many organisations that one could belong to but it is worth doing your research before signing up as many will charge you an annual fee and as a business you will want to make sure that your membership pays for itself, hopefully many times over.

In this book, I am not going to attempt to list all the organisations that are available as this would be a major task and indeed would need a separate book to capture all the data.

However, what I can do is list down those organisations that I have belonged to, had associations with or think would be useful for further consideration.

Organisations:

- FSB (Federation of Small Businesses)
- Chamber of Commerce (local to you)
- Professional bodies (of your chosen profession, in my case The Institute of Credit Management, FCIB finance and international business)
- Trade bodies (various)
- Networking groups (various)
- Technology groups (e.g. SAP)
- Enterprise groups (e.g. Marketing Derby)
- LinkedIn groups (Marketing, Consultancy, Strategy, CFO, Tech, Project Management, etc.)

Remember one day you may get asked to deliver a presentation or deliver a speech about your specialist subject matter, as an expert, and get paid for doing it.

Could you really now be on the paid speech circuit? Yes, you really could achieve this if it is what you want to do.

Project management methodology:

There are many project management methodologies out there today, but I have developed my own which can be best described as being like a lighter form of Prince 2.

When I started out on my independent story, I had only previously managed small projects while working for organisations in permanent operational roles and at that time I had never heard of Prince2. These projects were simply managed on the desire to get the job done, making sure that items where correctly documented and effective communications where taking place.

In these early days, it did not occur to me that there needed to be a set project management methodology as it surely was just the application of common sense that would get the job done. However, that's the thing with the modern world today that everything needs to be labelled and put in a box called a methodology so that it can be studied and taught, when in my early days it was called common sense and just get on with it.

I have since realised over time that my mind is wired in a way that thinks everyone has both common sense and thinks in the same processed and organised way that I do. This I have learned is just not the case, and so the way in which I have conducted myself with process improvements and project management has always closely aligned to one or other project management methodologies and therefore I had considered it quite natural to implement a kind of light touch Prince2 methodology way before I ever realised it had a name.

I guess that project management just comes naturally to some of us and a set methodology is, therefore, more a tool for the client than for us so minded souls!

Don't get me wrong at this point. I am not rubbishing any of the established or new methodologies as I think they do act as an anchor for both the client and the programme/project manager and his project team.

What I am alluding to here is purely the way my mind works and that is to say in the project management way that seems to have been written down and captured by a number of the main project methodologies. It's just a pity I didn't think of writing mine down first and having the necessary wherewithal to promote it as the main methodology to follow.

Never mind!!

So anyway, I have since become a Prince2 practitioner in my own right just to prove that I could do it too under a prescribed project management methodology.

On one particular project where I was the project manager I found one publication very useful as a refresher for my particular way of thinking about and managing projects.

This publication is 'The project Manager, mastering the art of delivery' by Richard Newton and published by Prince Hall. In this book, there is a very good section that I think sums up my philosophy on project management.

Here the author suggests that it is the way you deal and interact with people rather than the methodology that separates good project managers from the average ones.

For me, the section perfectly captures the way I feel about project management and in fact independent consultancy and business as a whole.

You could simply summaries this as common sense!

Although this book does go on to describe in some detail how to manage a successful project, it is done in such a way that makes it a very compelling read.

This book seems, for me at least, to capture the essence of how to act professionally in business using a holistic approach and, of course, a great deal of common sense.

I say a highly recommended read.

How to conduct yourself in business and in life, giving respect to people you meet along the way, having thought for what you are doing and to conduct yourself with the utmost professionalism and integrity at all times is the essence of this book.

IR35:

I will only lightly touch on the subject of IR35 as it is subject that can be discussed at length with any qualified accountant or HRMC tax inspector. Which, indecently, I do suggest that you do before forming your own views on the subject. Remember to be informed is to be knowledgeable.

However, here is my take on it:

IR35 and the independent consultant:

IR35 is a very relevant subject for any independent consultant and interim managers and you should fully familiarise yourself with the latest rules and legislation from HMRC.

I am not an expert on this subject and therefore will not be giving any advice on whether you will fall inside or outside of the IR35 rules and guidelines but what I will say is do your homework, seek expert advice from your accountant and HRMC themselves and make sure you get adequate insurance cover from a reputable provider for any tax enquires from HRMC that my result from your day to day business activities.

The latest information on IR35 if you have not come across it before is:

New IR35 rules apply for tax purposes from 6 April 2013 where a worker provides their personal services to a client via an intermediary to fulfil the duties of an office and the income for those services has not already been subject to PAYE/NICs as employment income.

For NICs purposes, the IR35 rules have always applied to office-holders whose services are supplied to clients via an intermediary. This is because office-holders are regarded as 'employed earners' for the purposes of IR35 NICs legislation. This continues to be the case.

However, prior to 6 April 2013 the IR35 tax legislation only applied to office-holders when a worker would also have been regarded as an employee if engaged directly by the client. Therefore if the worker's only relationship with a client was as an office-holder, then the IR35 tax rules do not apply for any services performed before 6 April 2013.

The IR35 tax legislation has now changed and office-holders are brought within IR35 for tax purposes for services performed on or after 6 April 2013 undertaking the duties of an office. The amendment changes sub-section 49(1)(c) in Part 2, Chapter 8 of the Income Tax (Earnings and Pensions) Act 2003 for the tax year 2013-14 and subsequent tax years.

This article was taken directly from the website of HMRC

www.hmrc.gov.uk

I suggest you regularly review the HRMC website for the most current legislation and comments to keep yourself abreast of any updates and upcoming changes and developments is this area.

Whether you do fall inside or outside of the IR35 rules or not this will not prevent you from doing business as an independent consultant or interim management, but it will affect the way your accountant will have to treat your tax affairs and of course the value of tax that you will ultimately be paying to HMRC.

At the end of the day, my best advice is to get professional advice!

Take detailed notes when gathering information and data:

(You will need to rely on these throughout the project lifespan).

They say that the art of writing is disappearing with the ever increasing electronic media such as email, text messaging, same time and twitter but as an independent consultant I can quite categorically tell you that my note taking (in long hand as I never learnt the art of shorthand) has been ever present and one of the most important tools of any assignment.

Like everything these days there is some good material online or in books about the art of note taking or how to take great notes, so I am not intending to go into such detail here, but what I will share with you is my experiences of why great note taking has helped me in my career as an independent consultant and why it is so important to take, maintain and keep your notes for future use.

Well written and comprehensively captured notes, taken from interviews and meetings with your clients and representatives, enables you to understand and judge current opinion and feelings, allows you to capture insights and ideas and to formulate your own views and strategies. And let's not forget great notes will definitely throw up lots of questions that will form the basis of future interviews and assignment direction and strategies.

So let's recap. Great notes allow us to:

- Begin to understand
- Allows us to judge opinion and feelings
- Give us insights
- Give us ideas
- Formulate our views and strategies
- Will throw up lots of questions.

You're starting to see here that the assignments direction and strategies develop and grow with great note taking.

The thought that I always carry around with me is:

If you ask no questions, you get nothing in return!

So for me the other very important aspect of great note taking is to ask searching questions and plenty of them.

When asking your questions be persistent and keep asking until you have closed out the answer. You see that's another great tip, great note taking requires persistence in the note taker to get to the route of a point or issue and not give up.

Make sure that your notes are legible. It sounds obvious to state this, but it is easy to be in a hurry to scribble something down and on reading back to miss the point of what you were trying to capture because you cannot read your own handwriting.

If you have learnt how to use shorthand then that's a great way of capturing notes quickly but if you are like me and have to rely on long hand for your note taking then the best advice I can offer you is to take you time and use distraction techniques to give you some extra time to capture your notes.

All I mean by distraction techniques is simply asking additional questions, asking the interviewee to draw a diagram of a particular process, reaching for a drink, asking for a drink, stopping to blow your nose. There are many!

The point is that you want to give your mind time to think and to capture what the interviewee is telling you concisely for future use and eliminating any misunderstanding.

So to recap, the art of great note taking is:

- Ask searching questions and plenty of them
- Be persistent
- Take legible notes
- Use distraction techniques

- Ask the interviewee to draw a diagram representing the process.

To finish this section on note taking let's look back at the central question.

What's so important of taking great notes?

Once you have taken your notes, then these notes will form a view on the business you are looking at and then will form your whole strategy on how to manage the assignment moving forward.

These notes will also form a diary of notes over the course of the assignments you are working on and will be a great source of information in the future. This information can then be used in the future to write white papers, presentations and other material.

I make sure that I use quality note books and have four different coloured pens to write up my notes. These note books then form a kind of library of notes that I have written and collected over the years and can be used as an information depository.

All my hand written notes are typed up and stored on a computer hard drive so they can be easily accessible not just for the assignment they were taken from but for future reference too.

Section 5

Personal development

Introduction:

In this section, we will be looking at the things you can do to help yourself get to where you want to be.

We shall be looking at how you can acquire knowledge and become to be seen as an expert in your chosen field of expertise. Taking a look at the world of goals setting and how this can help you both personally and professionally reach new heights. Seeing how receiving testimonials for your work can help your marketing campaigns and some other useful stuff.

One of my best pieces of practical advice is and a top tip:

Top tip:

Don't re-invent the wheel, use what works. If there is a methodology or a piece of advice that you have been given and it has worked on a previous assignment, use it again and again. There is no point in trying to do and find new ways of working if what you already do works and brings you success.

Another top tip and something I personally wouldn't be without:

Top Tip:

Make sure you always have to hand a great cup of coffee. Not instant stuff, I'm talking about grinding beans and filtering your own. Over the years, I have found immense comfort in the participation of great coffee to help me along the way.

Learn, grow and become an expert:

One of the ways to be a high achiever as an independent consultant is to become or be perceived to be an expert.

Now, if you are not already an expert in your field then I realise this may take some time to achieve but achieve it must be your goal to reap the big rewards and the longevity in the independent business. Without an expert status, you will be in a pool of talent that is indistinguishable from the competition.

So, to set yourself apart from the competition, work out what it is, in your chosen field, that will make you unique and be able to market yourself as an expert.

I managed over time to become an expert in my chosen field by learning all I could from other experts and always to question the status quo. I was always willing to seek out the latest professional and industry thinking and with my own inner common sense professionalism turn this into what I felt was the best way forward. Granted, my ways were never radical thinking but my take on what was deemed to be best practice at the time and to enhance on this.

Only you will know how far you need to develop to become an expert in your chosen field but become it you must.

Some of the ways to make sure you are seen as an expert is to participate in your specific area of relevance.

By this, I mean contribute some news or research or be a member of an organisation to contribute to.

E.g.

- Write a whitepaper
- Become a committee member, ideally chairman
- Be on the board of a professional organisation
- Be a panel member at conferences
- Be a presenter at conferences and group meetings
- Be a regular contributor to blogs, trade and professional press and LinkedIn groups
- Attend conferences and contribute from the floor
- Find courses and workshops to attend to find out what is being talked about
- Use your network to discuss the latest trends and technologies.

It is a great idea if you find yourself between assignments to spend as much time as you can spare researching your professional sphere for ideas, the latest techniques and technologies to keep yourself up to speed and fully current with the latest ideas and trends.

I have a naturally inquisitive mind, so I love nothing more than to seek out and read new books and articles or to search online for relevant and interesting pieces of information. Information that might help me win that future contract, help me better market myself or develop my skills to be recognized as an expert.

You can never do enough reading and researching. What is it that they say? Knowledge is power!

So, get stuck in and never stop learning.

Goal setting:

In this section, we are going to look briefly at goal setting. I say briefly because there has been plenty written about this subject matter, and I am not going to re-invent the wheel here. Consequently I will recommend to you a particular favourite goal setting process of mine and share my techniques to set better goals and to succeed with them.

I will also provide to you the format that I use to set out my goals and aspirations.

One of my favourite goal setting gurus is Tony Robbins, so get hold of some of his material on this subject. It really is very inspiring stuff. In his goal setting audios, he goes into great depth about how to set and realise your goals. However, like everything in life, only you can make it happen, and it will only happen with dedication and hard work, coupled with a desire and drive to succeed.

I am not going to share with you here any of Tony's material as it it's widely available online but do seek it out.

Another favourite author of mine is Zig Ziglar. His book titled 'See you at the top' by Zig Ziglar and published by Pelican Publishing Company, is a particularly good read for goal's setting. In his book there is a whole section on goals and the purpose for goals which really opens your mind up to the importance of capturing what it is you are striving to achieve in your life.

So, from reading 'See you at the top', by Zig Ziglar, you can appreciate that goals are not just a simple list of dreams or desires, but a well thought through list of things that will improve your life and a comprehensively stated plan of how you will achieve them.

Not the easiest task in the world! But then if it easy we would all be millionaires and living in a utopian world.

This is all great stuff and between the two authors and authorities on goals and goal setting, Anthony Robins and Zig Ziglar, you will find all you need to on the process and techniques for setting your own personal and business goals.

I am not even going to try and compete with these two great teachers on the matter of goals setting but what I will share with you is how setting goals has been a big part of my life both personally and in business and to touch on the format I use to set my goals.

I have set myself goals for as long as I can remember, but it's only more recently, over the last 10 years or so that I have looked at goals setting more seriously and as part of my overall personal and business strategies.

When I look back at my goals that I have set myself over the past 5 to 10 years I am always pleasantly surprised at how many of them I have achieved. Now, it is open to question how many of these you would have achieved without setting yourself the specific goals, but I firmly believe not as many as you did with the goals setting process.

You see, the whole goal setting technique is there so you have to think about what it is you want out of life, as a whole, and by recording this and stating them as your goals, you are already setting in motion the path to achievement.

Over the last 10 years I have set goals in all sorts of areas of my life from business to family and from recreation to learning. I have found the goals setting process focuses the mind on what it is that you really want and effectively hard-wires your brain to make sure you do things to achieve them.

So let's now have a brief look at my own goal setting technique.

My goals setting technique:

The first thing to say about goal setting is that the goals themselves should be all encompassing goals. By this, I mean that they cannot just be your business goals along but also need to address your personal and family goals too. After all, they are all connected and so need to be looked at holistically.

Therefore, when I look at my goal setting there are the following headings:

- Personal goals
- Family & relationship gaols
- Health & energy goals
- Financial goals
- Business & career goals
- Ideas goals (things that need further research).

Taken together these will form your life goals which in turn will help you focus on what's important in your life and enable you to achieve a work-life balance that works for you.

I personally find it impossible to set business goals in isolation as there are always the other elements that will be affected and vice versa.

I am not going to delve into any current detail on my specific goals under each heading as these are personal to me just like yours will be personal to you. Of course, they will depend on whether you are in a relationship if you have children and all manner of other elements in your life that are unique to you.

Suffice it to say that taken in isolation the list of goals are worth less than when they are taken together as a whole.

Top Tip:

Be holistic with your goal setting.

The last item on my goal setting list is something I call 'IDEAS.'

Here I look at all the things that I have thought would be great to do, ideas for businesses and things that in the future might we worth a go but are a bit beyond my current goal setting focus.

Some of my items under this heading are great business ideas that I have not yet had time to research but want to capture for future reference. Under this example, I currently have about 12 ideas pending further consideration.

So last but not least, I make sure that I try and capture a picture representation of some of my more materialistic goals to make me focus on the prize. Be it an expensive car, exotic holiday destination or item of jewellery.

Have fun setting your goals and see just how well you will do in achieving them over the next 12 to 24 months. You may even surprise yourself!

Testimonials:

Testimonials are just as much an essential part of your marketing strategy as anything else you do to promote yourself as an independent consultant.

It is always my objective to receive a testimonial from every client that I work with as this then builds up to quite a substantial file of praise in your work, and we all like to be loved, don't we!

I always remember the advice I was given early on in my career from one independent consultant I met while attending a particular interesting conference on 'building business through effective marketing strategies', (it was actually very interesting), and it was this:

'Never wait until you are due to complete an assignment to request a testimonial from your client'.

'Make sure, once you have identified who in the organisation the main decision maker is, that you impress them and request early (may be half way through your assignment) your desire for a testimonial when you complete your work'.

Since this simple piece of advice, I have always tried to do this and have always received a positive response to my early requests. Quite a few of my clients have indicated to me that it was a good idea to ask this question early and thereby fostering an early dialogue which made them think more thoroughly what it was that you were doing to improve and raise standards in their organisations and the value that you where personally adding.

I am, pleased to say that I have never had a negative testimonial.

Below I have listed a few examples of testimonials I have received over the years as an independent consultant:

Testimonials received:

'I have known Nigel for many years from when he was a Credit Manager in the information technology sector through to him becoming an independent consultant and business owner. He is a true professional in all he does, and I would have no hesitation in recommending him'.
Director, consulting firm and member of the ICM Advisory Council & Executive Board.

'Nigel brought the required organisation and project management skills at a critical juncture in the development of

our brand. He oversaw a major review of all aspects of our accounting department and established a strategic plan of action which resulted in the successful conclusion to the project. On the personal front, Nigel is professional and dedicated with excellent interpersonal skills'.
CFO, plc.

'I worked with Nigel at a global outsourcing organisation on a shared services project while implementing a new ERP system into their global back office functions. His extensive knowledge and experience in his specialist field and input into the best practice process design was impressive. He is very personable and easy to work with, and I would be happy to recommend him.'
Independent Consultant.

'Nigel worked as an independent consultant through me on a business critical project for a large global client of mine. The client's demands were nothing short of challenging, but Nigel managed to deliver the desired results and add value to their business with an extremely high level of integrity and professionalism. He is a highly analytical person with very strong business partnering skills required to get results. I have no doubt that Nigel would be a considerable asset to any business he engages with.'
International Head -hunter.

'I've known Nigel for many years now and during this time he has demonstrated that he has a detailed knowledge and experience in credit and receivables management and the order to cash cycle. While working with us, his contribution to our working capital consulting team was highly valued, and he became our resident credit risk best practice leader. Nigel is a real professional, dedicated to delivering high quality work, and someone my colleagues and I enjoyed working with.'
Director, Big Four accounting firm.

'Nigel has a deep understanding of credit management best practice, which he has been able to draw upon in working with our teams around the world to redesign our back office processes. He has a relaxed, but engaging working style that has allowed him to move things forward and get consensus. The challenge now will be to drive the project forward to implementation. There are also opportunities to broaden the scope of this intervention to address other issues within our global order to cash process.'
CFO, Global plc.

'Nigel has done a great job for us and it will be sad to see him go with so much knowledge of our organisation. I would happily recommend him for future assignments with other clients and would be happy to take him on if a new role comes up in the future.'
Group Finance Controller, Global plc.

'Nigel has extensive knowledge and experience in the field of order to cash process design and he has brought this to bear in setting up our global credit management processes. He is personable and easy to work with but remains focused to achieving objectives quickly. I would use his services in the future'.

Head of Group Information, UK plc.

'Nigel is an order to cash process implementation expert within financial shared service organisations. He has achieved excellent results for us.' Managing partner, Recruitment Agent.

These testimonials are just a few I have chosen to share with you to illustrate the power of acquiring them. There is nothing better to place on your website or in any marketing material than other peoples' recommendations. It provides potential clients with a sense or surety and comfort that they are not taking a risk on hiring you and your services.

This is particularly true if you can get senior executive endorsement i.e. CEO, CFO, COO, CIO, from large and well known corporations.

I have, over the past 15 years of independent consultancy, won several repeat business contracts and won a number of contracts via recommendations directly linked to testimonials.

So these contracts don't have to be only with direct leads, it is just as relevant for winning work via agencies too.

So there is no doubting that it works.

So, if you are in an assignment now or when you start you next one, don't be shy and be sure you get a testimonial.

After all, it's free and a very powerful marketing tool.

Glossary of top tips:

Chronological list of top tips given throughout the book:

Top tips from Section 1:

Be seen to be delivering something at least every two weeks.

Don't stick so close to the terms of engagement that you miss out on other opportunities to make process improvements and change working practices.

Always highlight process deficiencies as soon as you have verified them to the senior management of your client.

Top tips from Section 2:

One very important aspect of dealing with agents and head-hunters is to make sure that they are fully aware of your resume. Make sure that your resume is fully up to date and is focused on relevant information only (there is no need for padding just pinpoint your key experience and skills) and markets you effectively. Don't think of your resume as a simple CV, it is your main marketing tool so spend time getting it right, and you will reap the rewards.

Another tip is to identify and comment on future plans (i.e. make sure they know if you have decided to move into another area of interest that may not be immediately evident from your past assignments) and communicate this to your agent or head-hunter so they can add this to their search criteria.

So my advice to you is to get out there and network with your peers and competitors to expand greatly your client network and service offering which over time will elevate your own organisation as one that 'can do' rather than 'can't do!'

Don't limit yourself to the obvious networking opportunities.

Remember at all times to take into account the costs of running your business and the expense necessary to perform the contract or assignment in question. After all, you are in the business of making a profit and you must have a clear idea at all times of your profit margin.

Never let yourself be compromised in any way by giving others in the organisation the opportunity to muddy your name because mud sticks and you will be out on your ear before you can say 'independent consultant'.

Make sure your client knows your terms and conditions of business so that any conflicts are dealt with before the assignment starts. This will avert any disagreements later on.

Make the agents want to do business with you, because you offer them the best profit solution.

Top tips from Section 3:

There is no place in the independent consultants' armory for being arrogant, cocky or outspoken in an overly negative way.

As an independent consultant or interim manager, reputation is everything.

You must separate your personal views from those of the clients' business requirements, their culture and vision that they have for the business moving forward.

Top tips from Section 4:

Have a least two pre-prepared presentations formats ready when starting a new assignment.

Remember at all times when delivering a presentation to speak clearly, be heard and offer the facts in a visually appealing way while at all times engaging with your audience so that you don't lose them to boredom.

Don't underestimate the power of belonging to organisations and putting yourself forward to sit on the committee. It can really elevate your standing in your profession and industry.

Top tips from Section 5:

Don't re-invent the wheel, use what works. If there is a methodology or a piece of advice that you have been given and used before and it has worked on a previous assignment, use it again and again. There is no point in trying to do and find new ways of working if what you already do works and brings you success.

Make sure you always have to hand a great cup of coffee. Not instant stuff, I'm talking about grinding beans and filtering your own. Over the years, I have found great comfort in the participation of great coffee to help me along the way.

Be holistic with your goal setting.

Not 'The End', but just the beginning!

Next steps:

Going Independent can be a very liberating career choice.

If you would like more information about becoming an independent consultant and learning how I can help you achieve your goals, please feel free to connect with me on LinkedIn at http://uk.linkedin.com/in/nigeljhunt/ or Email me at **nigel@crestwayconsultants.co.uk**

Once we have established your particular goals and development needs, we can then tailor a course of coaching especially for you.

I look forward to hearing from you.

Notes:

Notes:

Notes:

Notes:

Notes: